# HOW TO **WOW**

# HOW TO
# WOW

Proven Strategies for
Selling Your [Brilliant] Self
in Any Situation

# Frances Cole Jones

Ballantine Books New York

2009 Ballantine Books Trade Paperback Edition

Copyright © 2008 by Frances Cole Jones

Published in the United States by Ballantine Books, an imprint of The Random
House Publishing Group, a division of Random House, Inc., New York.

BALLANTINE and colophon are registered trademarks of Random House, Inc.

Originally published in hardcover in the United States by Ballantine Books,
an imprint of The Random House Publishing Group, a division of
Random House, Inc., in 2008.

LIBRARY OF CONGRESS CATALOGING-IN-PUBLICATION DATA
Jones, Frances Cole.
    How to wow : proven strategies for selling your [billiant] self
in any situation / Frances Cole Jones.
        p.   cm.
    Includes bibliographical references.
    ISBN 978-0-345-50179-0
    1. Business communication.   2. Business presentations.   3. Interpersonal
relations.   4. Self-presentation.   I. Title.

    HF5718.J582 2008
    658.4'5—dc22        2007043454

Printed in the United States of America

www.ballantinebooks.com

9 8 7 6 5 4

*This book is dedicated to
Sri K. Pattabhi Jois*

*With gratitude and joy*

*and to my family
with much love*

# Contents

## CHAPTER FOUR
## Interview to a Kill:
### Stress-Free Job Interviewing                                81

## CHAPTER FIVE
## Stand and Deliver:
### Giving Speeches That Bring People to Their Feet            102

### CHAPTER SIX
## Pointed PowerPoint:
### Making PowerPoint Powerful                          **132**

## CHAPTER SEVEN
## Put It in Writing:
## But Before You Do . . .

## CHAPTER EIGHT
## Oh So Social:
## Making the Most of Your Social Interactions

CHAPTER NINE

## The Fine Points of Verbal Finesse:

### Answers to Questions, and Question and Answer 189

# Introduction

How often have you left an interview, a meeting, a presentation, an audition, thinking, "That's it! I nailed it!" only to discover you didn't get the job, the client, the account, the funding, the part?

Alternatively, how often have you left with a bad case of the "if only's"?

For me, there's nothing worse.

And today, due to the speed of the world we live in, these thoughts are compounded by the fact that we're rarely off duty. An elevator ride with our CEO turns into an impromptu presentation, our lunch date becomes a job interview, our conversation at a cocktail party sets the stage for a potential business merger.

But what if I told you that it's possible to be far more in command of how you're perceived than you currently realize? That you have far more control—in situations that are seemingly out of your control—than you know? That there are proven strategies that will leave your audience, interviewer, or whomever you are aiming to impress, thinking, "Now *that's* someone I want to work with"?

The name of my company is Cole Media Management, and I'm hired on a daily basis by individual clients and corporations to teach their executives and employees these valuable strategies.

Over the years Cole Media Management has been in business, I have met with hundreds of clients, across a spectrum of industries, preparing for everything from job interviews to sales meetings, appearances on *Oprah* to IPO road shows where they'll be asking for a billion (yes, that "B" is correct) dollars.

Every client, every situation is, of course, different, but regardless of the details of the situation, if you aren't getting the response you want, or expect, you need to look at your message and—just as important—at *how* you are expressing that message. Often, with just a few adjustments, you can go from a near miss to a slam dunk, from a "that was nice" presentation to one that knocks their socks off, from a mediocre meeting to one that fires up each and every participant.

The thing is, when you want to make a good impression no detail is too small. No amount of advance preparation is too much. No word choice is unimportant. The shirt you wear, the chair you sit in, the thank-you note you write afterward should all be carefully considered, and ultimately compound the impression of someone who's calm, confident, and in-command.

I present the information in *How to Wow* in a one- to two-page "search-and-destroy" format to make it easy for you to find the information needed in your situation—meeting, lunch, job interview, speech, PowerPoint presentation—so you can begin employing it, and enjoying the benefits of it, immediately. Then, when there's time to browse, you can wend your way through the other sections.

The strategies I offer come from a spectrum of modalities and, aside from the general principles discussed in chapter one, the information I offer my clients, and you, is yours to pick and choose from. There are no "rules" because I recognize that, as with my clients, each of you comes to the table with a unique set of attributes and circumstances. More important, I know each of you is smart enough to know what will work for you and your circumstances: what will help give you the confidence to speak your mind in a meeting, motivate your team under deadline, or negotiate your business deal over pasta puttanesca.

I will know I've succeeded when you begin to doubt your doubts—to be confident in your confidence. Because when you are, you are free to be enthusiastic, committed, authentic.

The you that you know yourself to be when you're at your best.

Because that's where the *wow* is.

# HOW TO **WOW**

## CHAPTER ONE

# Don't Leave Home Without Them:
## The Nonnegotiable General Principles

I began presenting myself early and, if I remember correctly, somewhat reluctantly.

When my siblings and I were in the age range of three to six, my father would line us up in the living room before a cocktail party and make us practice shaking hands with him before the guests arrived. (The Von Trapp family had nothing on us.) I still remember him looming over me, pumping my hand up and down while saying, "Look me in the eye, look me in the eye, look me in the eye . . ."

While I may not have enjoyed those impromptu personal presentation sessions, their effect was beneficial. To this day, I have a super handshake, and definitely look people in the eye when I greet them.

As with looking someone in the eye, there are some elements to presenting yourself that are nonnegotiable. Regardless of the situation, these fundamentals are necessary in order to make a strong and lasting impression. Whether you are presenting to one or one hundred—at a lunch, on the phone, with a speech or PowerPoint presentation—they will always be beneficial. These nonnegotiable principles are presented here. If you read or do nothing else in this book, incorporating these foundational elements into your daily communication and interaction will guarantee instantaneous, positive results in how people respond to you.

## Dearly Beloved Data Lovers

The following statistic, from a study done by Albert Mehrabian, Professor Emeritus of psychology at UCLA, is among the first things I tell every client. Known as the "7%—38%—55% Rule" it states that there are three elements to any face-to-face communication: words, tone of voice, and body language, and we are influenced by these things as follows:

- 7 percent of our influence comes from the words we say.
- 38 percent from our tonal quality while saying it.
- 55 percent by what our body is doing while we're saying it.

What does this mean? So often we think presentation and communication are about the words we say. In fact, it's often far more about *how* we say them, and what our body is doing *while* we are saying them.

For example, we've all been introduced to the person who says, "Nice to meet you" with a fishy hand, a nominal smile, and an over-our-shoulder-to-see-if-someone-more-interesting/important/attractive-is-coming-in-the-room gaze. Contrast that with meeting someone who's genuinely delighted to meet you.

Same words, very different message.

My goal in telling you this is to help you begin to consider the global impact of your message—to understand the importance of managing every aspect of your presentation style.

- Knowing that listeners often remember just 7 percent of the words you say will remind you to choose language that's precise, colorful, and concise.
- Knowing that 38 percent of your impact comes from your tonal quality will reinforce the importance of having your tone match your message: be authoritative, commanding, persuasive, entertaining, etc, depending on your objective.
- Knowing that 55 percent of your impact comes from what your

body is doing while you are speaking will encourage you to focus on how you can best express commitment to, and enthusiasm for, what you are saying through your facial expressions, posture, and gestures.

Breaking down your message in this way makes it much easier to figure out what you need to do to capture your listener's attention. You can ask yourself:

- Is my language flabby?
- Do I sound happy when I'm giving good news, and genuinely sorry when I'm apologizing?
- If I were on television—and the sound was off—would someone walking by the TV know from my body language that I was enthusiastic about, or committed to, what I was saying?

As with anything, the first step to creating effective change is awareness. Now that you have a greater understanding of the factors in play when you present yourself, you can begin to pick and choose, strengthen or minimize, bump up or play down each element to achieve the results you desire.

## Tell Me a Story

As children, we all felt the power of storytelling, its ability to transport us to another place and time. As adults, we feel it when we're in the grip of a masterful book or movie. Using stories when speaking has the same effect on your listeners, *and* the added bonus of helping you retain and commit to the message you want to deliver.

Two of the most frequent questions I get from new clients are "How can I get rid of filler words like 'um' and 'uh'?" and "What should I do with my hands?" Embedding their answers in stories solves both these problems. Think about it, when was the last time you were wrapped up in telling your best friend or coworker your latest grievance against your spouse or your boss *and* simultaneously using filler words or worrying about what your hands were doing? It's simply not possible.

An important point to remember in this is that the story doesn't have to be long to be effective. I heard a great example of this on a morning talk show. The segment was "The best new minivans." The speaker said, "This minivan is so big you can drive six kids to soccer practice, pick up some wood from the lumberyard on the way home, and build a tree house with them that afternoon."

Excellent storytelling, and not a stray "um" to be found.

How can you find the shorthand story that will make you memorable? The quickest way is to speak from your own experience—which will provide you with colorful, heartfelt examples—while simultaneously acknowledging your listener's experience, situation, or expertise. Ask yourself, "Why do I care?" Then ask yourself, "Why should they care?" Once you have the answers to those questions, you'll have a great story.

## "My name is Bond"

From time to time I teach presentation skills seminars for new hires at large corporations. Inevitably, at some point during my pitch to a new firm, I hear, "Yes, but most of the time all these kids get to say in meetings is their name." "*All?*" is my response. (At this point, I know the person I'm speaking to might benefit from some presentation skills training, too.) Why? Because you are never "just" saying your name. Presenting the self is an opportunity.

The best example of this I can think of is, "My name is Bond. James Bond."

Regardless of who's saying it, Roger Moore, Sean Connery, or Daniel Craig, within that one sentence we hear a world of possibility.

In the same way, then, whenever you introduce yourself you need to say your name with such panache that your listener:

- remembers it.
- is left thinking, "Wow, that guy was impressive. . . . Am I supposed to know him?"
- is so knocked out by your "presentation" he wants to get to know you better.

If it helps, you can imagine you have "Q" as your backup, an Aston Martin as your getaway car, and a cold martini waiting at home.

So whether you are sitting in an executive board meeting, standing up at the PTA, or shaking hands in an elevator, always give your name the VIP treatment that flags it as a "Marquee Name" for those around you, leaving them alive to the possibilities and opportunities that knowing you offers them.

## Useless Modifiers Are Just That

*"It's great, it's amazing, it's incredible, it's so cool . . ."*

Can you tell from the above whether it's your boss talking about the new hotel he just stayed in, your coworker telling you about her new car, or your teenager describing the new telephone he wants you to get him?

Nope.

The only way we'll believe your experience or product or skill set is amazing is if you tell us *why*. And it's not enough to include the answers to the standard reporters' questions: who, what, where, when, and why. We need to know—what did you see? Hear? Touch? Taste? Smell? How did it make you feel? What did it remind you of?

A good place to see people practicing this is on cooking shows. Because we can't smell or taste the food, these chefs have to describe those elements in detail. "The smell of these cookies baking reminds me of sitting on my Grandma's back porch watching the laundry dry on the line . . ."

As with most things, this is a skill that comes with practice. Initially, your practice will just be to notice when others are falling back

> **An Utterly Unscientifically Chosen List of Fifteen Words That Say Nothing at All**
>
> | | |
> |---|---|
> | Amazing | Great |
> | Awesome | Hard |
> | Boring | Incredible |
> | Cool | Interesting |
> | Exciting | Nice |
> | Extraordinary | Terrific |
> | Fun | Wonderful |
> | Good | |

on "great," "amazing," "incredible." One place I hear this a lot is with actor interviews. A common interview question actors are asked when their new movie opens is, "What was it like to work with so-and-so director/ fellow actor?" In these moments, unless there's been some coaching, many actors fall back on, "He was great." "She was amazing . . ." Granted these stock responses are understandable. They don't want to say, "Oh my goodness, I was in *hell.*" What, then, could they do instead? What's a safe answer that also highlights their intelligence? Tell us a story: "One thing I didn't expect was his wicked sense of humor. He played the most ridiculous jokes on the entire cast. For example, one day he . . ." etc.

Once you've spent some time observing others, you will want to begin to notice your own habits. How was your day? Your sandwich? The movie? Have your friends challenge you. Can you get through each of their questions without using a single useless modifier? Once you accept the challenge, you'll discover that it's great fun—and that they've started referring to you as a master storyteller.

## The All-Important Diaphragm

While this tip is important for both sexes, it's particularly important for women as we tend to have higher—and subsequently less authoritative—voices.

To naturally lower your voice, you want to speak from your diaphragm. What does this mean? Or, more accurately, what does this sound like?

Well, as mentioned, it naturally moves your voice into a lower register. If you think you have problems with sounding "nasal" this solves those, too.

What does it look like? When you are speaking from your diaphragm, your abdomen naturally moves in and out with the movement of your diaphragm. A quick way to check if this is happening is to place your hand on your abdomen and see if it's moving in and out while you speak. If it's not, you need to begin accessing your diaphragm. (One of my favorite coaching moments was having a male client say, "But I don't think men have one of those." Tackling that was a task far beyond my pay grade. . . .)

How to do this? An easy way is to lie on the floor, put a telephone book on your stomach, and breathe in and out as deeply as you can. You want to be able to see the phone book move up and down . . . a lot. If it's not, keep breathing. It may take a minute or two, as many of us have become used to our shallow breathing.

Once you're comfortable with this, stand up, place your hand on your stomach and say a few practice sentences. The results are immediate. Your body will naturally retain this diaphragmatic breathing for a minute or so; your voice will have a lovely resonance.

Now that you're aware of the difference this makes, make it a habit to check in with yourself and, if you notice your abdomen's not moving, recalibrate. This doesn't mean getting out the phone book every single time, just keeping your hands on your abdomen and breathing deeply until they are moving in and out with your breath. Over time, it will become second nature—you'll be uncomfortable speaking any other way.

Additionally—and these are great "gifts with purchase"—you'll be calming your nervous system, strengthening your respiratory system, and releasing both stress and toxins . . . all while appearing unflappable.

## "You're such a bad dog . . ."

I imagine most of us have had the experience of having a friend's dog jump on us while its owner coos, "Oh, you're such a bad dog . . . you're the worst dog in the world."

Does the dog know he's being indescribably awful? Absolutely not. (Does your friend know how crazy-making this can be? Probably not.) Why? Because her tone and her words don't match.

I see the same thing happening when no canines are present. A speaker will get to the podium and say, "I'm so happy to be here today" while putting down his notes, adjusting his mic, smoothing down his tie . . . all the while looking anything but happy. You'll be introduced to someone at a cocktail party who will say, "Great to meet you," while looking over your shoulder to see if someone they'd prefer to meet is behind you. Your spouse will say, "I love you too, honey," without looking up from the paper. . . .

Here's the thing: You've got to put the "happy" into "happy." If you're happy to be there, you have to sound happy. Your eyes have to look happy. Your body has to express happy. If someone in the audience can't hear the words you're saying, they should still know you're communicating "happy." If you're introduced to someone and say, "Great to meet you," it's important that they are left thinking that you think it actually is great to meet them. And if you tell someone you love her, you want her to leave for the day with that warm, fuzzy feeling.

What happens when there's a disconnect between your words and your expression of them? Well, depending on the person's tone, you might end up flagging him as anything from nervous to self-absorbed to "too cool for school" to untruthful. None of which make a favorable impression.

I'm not saying it's easy to stay present for every introduction, but I am saying it makes a difference—it distinguishes you in others' minds. The other reason I recommend this is that, as Aristotle said, "We are what we repeatedly do. Excellence, then, is not an act but a habit." The habit of bringing your full attention to the words you say—embodying them for your listener—means that in the moments when the stakes are high because you're meeting your prospective boss, investor, fiancé, you'll be ready.

## Your Most Persuasive Words

In 1970, Yale University did a study of the most persuasive words in the English language. They claim the *most* persuasive word in the English language is "you."

Surprised?

Funnily enough, I'm guessing that once you think about it, you're not. We all like to be acknowledged and appreciated. We all like to know we count.

How can knowing this work for you?

When I work with clients, I advise them to both frame their responses in terms of their audience's interests—"What's in it for you?"—and to literally use the word "you" a lot.

Here's an example: I was working on an IPO show down in Mexico and my client kept saying, "And the Mexican constituency can use this technology to do X, Y, Z . . ."

Huh? No one thinks of themselves in the third person. (Except, perhaps, royalty of some sort . . . "Her Majesty's Grace will do as she pleases" . . . But I digress . . .)

I asked him to change it to, "And you can use this technology to do . . ."

Ah! Me?? *I* can? *Now* I'm interested . . .

You see?

What are the remaining eleven words on the Most Persuasive Words List?

| | |
|---|---|
| 2. Money | 8. Safety |
| 3. Save | 9. Love |
| 4. New | 10. Discovery |
| 5. Results | 11. Proven |
| 6. Health | 12. Guarantee |
| 7. Easy | |

Interesting, right? My clients generally think so. In fact, I have one firm that plays the "Who can get the most of these words into their presentation?" game during every meeting. Because they are financial-types, the word "love" was giving them trouble. The day they solved this they were so proud they called me up. Their solution? When they get to a particularly intricate slide on their Power-Point handouts, they say, "I love this slide!"

## What to Wear? What to Wear?

For many of us, this question can suck up a lot of time and attention on a regular day. When you throw in an important meeting, a presentation, an appearance in traffic court, or a cocktail party with the ever-helpful phrase "Festive Dress" in the corner of the invitation,

### I Before You

While using "you" is a wonderful way to engage your listener, reassuring him that you are giving his interests and/or concerns equal weight with your own, it's not a useful word to throw around during a heated discussion, an argument, a problem-solving conversation . . . call it what you will. In those situations, beginning sentences with, "You always/You said/You think/Why can't you?" generally doesn't help things along. Depending on the context and tone, phrasing things in this way can convey an enormous amount of hostility, resentment, disparagement.

Given that, I recommend instead putting "I" before "you." For example:

- "You agreed to be in charge of X," becomes, "As I remember our conversation, you agreed to be in charge of X."

- "You said you'd provide Y—which is why I agreed to meet you halfway," becomes, "When I agreed to meet you halfway, my understanding was that you were going to be providing Y."

- "When you say things like Z, I'm not sure you're willing to resolve this," becomes, "When I hear words like Z, I'm not sure you want to resolve this," etc.

Too often, beginning with "you" packs too much of a punch.

you can really ramp up the suck-time. As you know, whole books and countless magazines devote themselves to this conversation. My goal here is just to put some parameters in place so that you can feel confident and comfortable in any situation.

In every case, you are going to want to take your cue from the probable dress code of your host, the time of day, and your intention: to inspire confidence, to impress, to promote trust, etc.

For example, recently I had a day when I had two very different meetings. In the morning I was meeting with a state-run agency whose mission is to enforce safety code and whose goal was to increase transparency with the public. For them, I wore tailored pants, a button-down shirt, flat shoes, and carried a functional bag. My goal was to reassure them that I understood their audience—mass, their budget—modest, and their mission—accessibility. That afternoon, I had a pitch meeting for new business with a Latin American company. Having researched them on the Web, my guess was that they would respond to a very different look, that it was important for me to break out higher heels and a few designer labels. For them, this way of dressing was reassuring; for my morning client, it would have been off-putting.

In a business setting, my overarching recommendation regarding clothing is that it be constructed—i.e., well-tailored. This means that shirts should have a collar and cuffs. For men, this is because it's unlikely they will be in a business setting that might allow for a T-shirt; for women, this is because it's all too easy for an unconstructed shirt to end up looking like a leotard. The fact that both the Gap and Banana Republic have now mastered the stretch/no-iron fabric necessary to make these clothes washer- and dryer-compatible is genius. They're both affordable and user-friendly.

If you want to get something more distinctive, please remember that "cheap is expensive and expensive is cheap." In other words, while there have been moments when I've flipped over a price tag and started to laugh, thinking, "They want *that* much money for black pants?" the fact remains that black pants are a staple of any wardrobe and that investing in one beautiful pair that isn't going to begin to fray or stretch or stain after a year makes a lot more sense than buying a new pair every eight months or so. If you want to invest in a beautiful shirt, the same is true. If and when you do, I recommend that it be blue. Why? Because blue looks good on most people, photographs best, and studies have shown it promotes trust. Within the spectrum of possible shades of blue, I recommend a French, or cornflower, blue.

"But," you may be thinking, "I look *great* in white or pink or yellow." That may be true. I'm only saying that if your budget is limited, blue is a fail-safe option.

In terms of your next big business-wear investment, I think it has to be in a really good handbag or briefcase. Once again, I know that "really good" can often lead to sticker-shock, but these items, well cared for, will literally last you a lifetime. If you can only afford one, this is not the time to pick something to express your personality. I know green reptile skin has a place, but—aside from the reptiles originally wearing it—it doesn't really work day to day.

After that, if your budget stretches to it, I suggest investing in a good watch. Again, it can seem like a small thing but, as they say, "the devil's in the details." The fact that you've gone to the trouble to do this will speak volumes to others.

For social situations, if you are unsure about the possible dress code—for example, dresses vs pants for women, open shirts or neckties for men—*call your host or hostess and ask*. A good host will always want a guest to feel comfortable. He or she would much rather field a few inquiries than know a guest feels out of place. After that, my only recommendation is that your choice be both body and age-appropriate. No one wants to see a man being throttled by his tie, or a woman vacuum-packed into an outfit that would be more appropriate on an MTV spring break special.

Ultimately, whether you are a willing or unwilling slave to fashion, it pays to spend the time and the money to make the best possible choice for you and your situation. If it helps, think of it as appropriate costuming. We all know how jarring it is to be watching a period drama and notice someone's twenty-first-century innovation—

whether it be a push-up bra, Rolex, or Reeboks. The same is true here: You never want your wardrobe to detract from the message you have chosen to convey.

## Your Nerves Are in Your Neck

A lot of people are nervous about speaking in public. When I ask them what happens to them physically, they'll often tell me, "I get short of breath" or "I feel sick to my stomach." When I hear this, I ask them to bend over . . . and let their head hang freely. (I'll bet you didn't think that's where that sentence was going . . .)

The reason for this is that the nerves that control your digestion and respiration attach at your C3 and C4 vertebrae—in other words, in the middle of the back of your neck. When we get tense, the muscles in our necks tend to bunch up around these nerves, causing them to double up on their duties; this leads to shallower breathing and an upset stomach. Bending at the waist and letting the head hang freely relaxes these muscles, which allows the nerves to relax.

Often when I talk about letting the head hang, I'll get people who bend over but continue to keep tension in their neck. Maybe it's from too many years of adopting this stance to tie their shoes—a place where you see a lot of neck tension. (Which is interesting, because after about age five most of us don't need to look at what we're doing when we tie our shoes. Nevertheless, we have held onto the habit of holding our head up to watch ourselves do this.) To check and see if you are keeping tension in your neck, place your fingers on the ridge at the base of your skull and gently, gently pull your head downward.

If you're not flexible, I recommend standing about a foot away from a wall and leaning your backside against the wall while you do this. Bend your knees, engage your abdomen, let your arms hang freely, allow the weight of your head to pull the head toward the floor.

Regardless of the position you adopt, you want to keep your

mouth closed and breathe through your nose. This particular way of breathing is important because breathing through our mouths tells our body we are in distress. Breathing through our nose calms our central nervous system. A way to help deepen your breathing is to lengthen your exhalation—not try to increase your inhalation. Why? Because your lungs will naturally rebound to replace the air you've exhaled. Simply trying to inhale more deeply is stressful for the body, and if you're in a nervous state to begin with, it contributes to possible hyperventilation.

When you are ready to stand up, bend your knees a bit more, keep your arms hanging like a rag doll and roll slowly up to stand, vertebra by vertebra. Your head should be the last thing you bring up. Once you're standing, shake your hands vigorously—from the shoulder, not from the wrist—as if you've gotten something stuck on them that you want to get off. Or, in this case, to rid yourself of adrenaline you want to get out.

A lot of people I've worked with have been *highly* resistant when I first asked them to do this. I even had a guy on one team who initially insisted on keeping his hands on the table while he did it and only bending forward enough to look as if he was shortsighted and trying to read papers on the table. Interestingly, it's this same team who now asks when I arrive, "Can we begin with stretching?" The reason for this is that it's an amazingly easy way to give yourself the feeling of having had an hour's nap in the middle of the day.

## Listen Up!

Of course, in addition to speaking, the other gigantic piece of communication is listening—a sadly underutilized art form.

One misapprehension people have about listening is that it doesn't require effort. They have ears. Therefore, they can hear someone speaking. Therefore, they are listening.

But that kind of listening is just called hearing.

Another misapprehension people have is that if they are very,

very involved in communicating their point of view, they are listening. In fact, they are just counting the seconds until the other person is finished speaking so they can continue talking.

That kind of listening is just called waiting.

A third misapprehension is that when we nod our head and smile as someone is speaking while our thoughts are a million miles away because we already "know" what they are going to say, that we are listening.

That kind of listening is just called phoning it in.

Reading these, it's possible you recognize some of these modes of "listening." In fact, it's possible that you, yourself, might have "listened" this way from time to time. I know I have. I also know that when I have, I've missed an extraordinary amount of the meaning behind what people were trying to say to me.

What can we do?

Winston Churchill said, "It takes courage to stand up and speak; it also takes courage to sit down and listen." I find this idea—that listening well requires as much from us as speaking well—wonderful. Whenever I've applied it, I know I've gotten very different results than I would have gotten if I had spent the time while someone was speaking just waiting to pipe up with my point of view.

However, the art form that is listening is, for me, best summed up in the following quote from the Indian philosopher, J. Krishnamurti:

"If you are listening to find out, then your mind is free, not committed to anything; it is very acute, sharp, alive, inquiring, curious, and therefore capable of discovery."

If you are listening to find out . . . This is the piece that gets lost. Sometimes because we aren't paying attention, sometimes because we are overanxious to tell our story, sometimes because we think we know what the other person is going to say. Whatever the reason, it's rare that we are truly *listening to find out*—but, as with so many things that are rare, it has a value that is beyond price.

## Dear Diary

This technique is something I learned when I was doing some work with Eric Butterworth, author of *The Creative Life*, and I am grateful to him for it.

While most of us no longer keep the kinds of diaries we did when we were teens, we remember the drill—writing a detailed account of what had occurred during our day. "Went to school, wore my favorite new T-shirt, saw X, she looked at me this way, I could tell she was thinking Y." Then this happened, then that happened . . . What I'm asking you to do with this exercise is, when you have a critical meeting or event or lunch the next day, write a diary entry *as if it is tomorrow*. Literally, "I got up. I wore X because it makes me feel more confident. I arrived at the office five minutes early and gave the receptionist my name. When Y came out, I got up unhurriedly but shook hands enthusiastically. We walked down to his office. I commented on his lovely view and accepted water when it was offered . . . ," etc, etc. Right up until "He walked me to the elevator, shook my hand, and said, 'It was such a pleasure to meet you. I look forward to working together.' After the elevator doors closed, I did a quick victory dance. Tonight, my friends are taking me out to celebrate. . . ."

While many people dismiss this kind of work as "magical thinking" I can assure you it has a place. One thing it does is to force you to consider exactly what you will be wearing, where you will be parking, how you will answer the tough questions, what questions you will ask, and how you will respond to those answers.

What people discover when they're asked to write it all out is how many things they haven't considered or, if they have considered them, breezed past, telling themselves, "Oh, I'll know what to do when that happens—but it probably won't happen." Forcing yourself to write it through moment by moment ensures you haven't left any plot holes.

The other benefit is substantiated by a study done at the University of Chicago. There a group of people were taken to a gym and asked to throw free throws. Afterward, they were divided into three sections.

One did no more practice. One group went to the gym and shot free throws for an hour a day for thirty days. The third group visualized shooting free throws for an hour a day for thirty days. At the end of the thirty days, they all came back to the gym and were retested. The group that hadn't practiced hadn't improved. The group that had physically done the practice had improved by 24 percent, the group that had visualized practicing had improved by 23 percent. . . .

That's "magic" I can get behind.

So, whether you believe in the potential benefit of visualization or not, I don't see any downside to going through the process of writing your "Diary Entry for Tomorrow." At worst, you'll have prepared thoroughly for succeeding. At best, you will succeed. Either way, you won't be able to reproach yourself for not doing enough. And this, to me, means you've already succeeded.

Finally—should you need further incentive—know that Albert Einstein, who I think we can all agree was a smart fellow, said, "The distinction between past, present, and future is just an illusion, however persistent."

## More Isn't Better. Better Is Better.

Here's the thing: my back didn't use to bend, and even now it doesn't bend easily. Not only do I come from an inflexible family, both physically and mentally, but I've spent a lot of years hunched over books, reading, reading. . . . I was never one of those seemingly happy-go-lucky girls turning cartwheels or doing walkovers on the beach or playground. Additionally, as is possible for many of you, a lot of time in recent years has been spent crouched over a computer. This hasn't helped.

What this meant was that when I tried my first backbend in yoga, I thought I was going to have to spend the rest of my life in traction. Once I realized I might still be able to walk upright, the challenge was on. I became obsessed with getting my back to bend. One day my teacher stopped me. "More isn't better," he said. "Better is better."

These became words to live by, both on the mat and in the office. Here's an example of what I mean:

Recently, I was working with a client who was creating a video for an advertising agency that wanted him to produce a ninety-second spot. Unfortunately, the directives they'd given him in terms of the financials available to him and the music they wanted included, precluded coming up with ninety seconds of truly creative material. At sixty seconds, the creative possibilities were tapped. Being a perfectionist, he was agitated by this.

"What you do," I said, "is tell them that 'more isn't better. Better is better.' "

He did, and it worked, because — as it's possible you will discover once you incorporate this idea into your world — most of the time it's the truth. Most presentations aren't better for being longer, most conference calls aren't better for being extended, most meetings aren't more productive because you spent more time in the room. It's just that in this age of super-sizing everything from hamburgers to automobiles, we've become addicted to the idea that more is better. I'm here to ask you to join my revolution, to tattoo on your brain, if not your backside, that "More isn't better. Better is better."

## "Because, because, because, because, because . . ."

The above title comes, of course, from "We're Off to See the Wizard" in *The Wizard of Oz.* Why were Dorothy & Co. going to see the wizard? "Because of the wonderful things he does." After all, depending on whom they asked, the wizard could do anything from give you a brain to dye your eyes to match your gown.

The trouble we sometimes run into is that when we're rushed, when we're distracted, when we think the answer is obvious, when we don't want to be questioned too closely, when we're nervous about getting our way, when we feel entitled to get our way . . . in all these scenarios, we often just announce what we want or need to have happen without including listeners in our decision-making process. We don't fill them in on the "because."

For example, perhaps you cut the line at the supermarket because you're late to pick your kids up from school and think that takes precedence over waiting behind others. Or perhaps your boss tells you that you've been chosen to go on a business trip that you know will upset the plans of your spouse, so when you get home you announce that change without explaining why because you think that will help you to avoid an argument. Or perhaps you have to ask your team to work overtime, and you make that request without giving them an explanation because you don't think it's something they'll understand, or something they need to know.

But here's a statistic it's important to note: social psychologist Ellen Langer did a study that showed that including listeners in the "because" of why something is happening increases their cooperation rate from 60 to 94 percent. I'll write that again and italicize it because I think it's so amazing: *it increases their cooperation rate from 60 to 94 percent.*

Here are a few examples of "because" turning things around in my life. When my friend Jill was very newly pregnant with twins we went to look at marble for her kitchen countertops. When we got to the shop, the guys there pointed us in the general direction of what we needed but weren't inclined to do more than that to help things along. The minute they heard that the reason we were nervous about shifting samples around was because Jill was pregnant, however, they couldn't have been more attentive—and more congratulatory! Thanks to the "because," we ended up having a lovely, memorable time in their store. Without the "because," it's likely things would have ended with our being frustrated, or their being resentful at our seeming helplessness.

I used to work in publishing. Once, when I was editing a manuscript, I asked an author to cut large sections of text that had become near and dear to him and, because I thought the "why" was obvious, I didn't include the "because." This ended in an extended phone conversation with a (rightfully) very upset author—one whose trust in me had been shaken by my seemingly offhand deletion of his work. Once the "because" of why I had made the cuts was explained to him, however, he was able to hear my reasoning and make the changes that strengthened the book.

When one of my clients realized he was going to have to ask his team to put in another twelve hours on a PowerPoint presentation they had only finished that afternoon—and which he was giving the next morning—he wasn't inclined to give them the "because"; his attitude was "They work for me. It's their job to do it. Besides, we don't have time." Convincing him that it was worth the hour it would take for me to talk them through the reasons behind the changes, however, meant we got their best work in the remaining eleven hours. Ultimately, even he agreed that his presentation was stronger for it.

So if you find yourself in a situation where you need someone's cooperation, best work, understanding, be sure you've included the "because." Because if you do, it's 94 percent likely you'll get the assistance or support you're looking for.

## Entrances and Exits

I'm a fairly avid yoga practitioner. Within the realm of various styles of yoga, I practice Ashtanga yoga. One of the key elements of the Ashtanga practice is that the poses are set up in series—primary through sixth—and within each series, the poses must be done in the same sequential order. Additionally, the entrance and exit to each pose is specifically choreographed. For instance, you enter some back bending poses with your hands on your hips and you enter others with your hands folded in front of your chest.

"Okay," you're thinking (or maybe "So what?"), "but how does this apply to me presenting myself?"

The reason I think it's not only applicable, but important, is that we are often so intensely focused on the event in question—the interview, the speech, the presentation, the meeting—that we forget the importance of how we enter and exit the situation. We neglect the niceties that grease the wheels: the name of our interviewer's assistant or the guy who's fitting us with our microphone, the thank-you to the bus person who fills our water glass or who takes our coat, the acknowledgment of the expertise of the person who wrote the PowerPoint presentation or created the marketing package that's going to help us to get the money, the contract, the position we want.

And these things are important.

They are important not just because they are the courtesies due to others, but because the ability to drop into the moment we are in, *when we are in it,* is an invaluable practice. If we are mentally rushing ahead all the time—handing off our coat, calling impatiently for the work we've asked to have created—then we won't be in the practice of being in the moment *during* our big moment. Our speeches will end with a "race to the finish line" that leaves our audiences bewildered, our meetings will be riddled with mini-misunderstandings since we've already begun contemplating who we're going to tap to do follow-up, our lunches will be punctuated by awkward silences as we consider how long we have to wait before broaching the "real" reason why we're there.

So the next time you are preparing for any type of meeting—whether it's with a colleague, a boss, a friend, a date—don't forget to factor in the importance of being present for your entrance and exit. It's a practice that benefits you, and those around you.

## Two Is One, and One Is None

This is a phrase my brother, a former captain in the Marine Corps, likes a lot, and it's one the military uses frequently. What this maxim does is turn the somewhat fatalistic "Murphy's Law" ("Whatever can go wrong, will go wrong") into something that you can do something about.

For example, at its most basic, it's about making sure that you put two pens into your pocket before a meeting, saving you the embarrassment of breaking out your legal pad prepared to take careful notes, and then having to say, "Um . . . my pen seems to be out of ink. May I please borrow one from you?"

## The 6 P's

Recently, a friend and I were hunting for a taxi late at night, in the *freezing* cold, on icy streets, each of us holding one of her children while wearing inappropriate footgear.

"I'll have to pay you back," I told her. "I have no cash on me."

"But I have no cash on me," she said.

Luckily we're old friends, so we started to laugh.

"What happened?" her son asked me as we slipped and slithered across Broadway toward the nearest bank.

"Your mother and I forgot the six P's." I told him. "In the Marine Corps, the six P's stand for: Prior Planning Prevents Piss-Poor Performance."

I figure it's never too early to start learning.

Because the truth is, pens fail; white shirts get spilled on (experienced consultants always pack an extra on overnight trips); and important papers get mislaid. If, however, before setting out for an important event, you think, "Two is one, and one is none," you're less likely to be caught out when Murphy's Law strikes.

Looked at another way, when you go into a meeting or an interview or a lunch, it reminds you that you need to have thought through at least two options for each choice you've made—from the answers to the questions you might get, to the possibilities for entrées you might order. In every case, knowing you have built out beyond Plans A and B to Plan C is going to give you an enormous amount of mental comfort.

If all of this seems a bit over the top, or (some might say) paranoid, consider another favorite expression of my brother's—courtesy of Henry Kissinger—which I've also found useful from time to time: "Paranoid is well informed."

## It's Easy to Make It Look Hard— What's Hard Is to Make It Look Easy

A few years ago I was dating a man who was kind of a big deal. This is not why I liked him. The reason I liked him was that in addition to being one of the most curious and open-minded people I've ever met, he was inevitably careful to make what he did seem easy, effortless, low-key. He had dropped the frenzy and the bluster that so often accompany people in high-pressure jobs.

Let me give you an example: over the two years we dated I was asked exactly once, "May I call you back this afternoon?" It seems his secretary had the vice president on the other line.

The vice president of the United States.

I said it would be okay.

Here's the thing: feeling important is fun. And lots and lots of us enjoy the sound of our own voices. (Heaven knows I do! And my friends would certainly back that up . . .) But one of the easiest ways to undermine people's confidence in you and your abilities is to keep drawing their attention to how hard you are working, how much you have to manage, how stressful your day was. Doing this can feel good to us—bolster our sense of who we are in the world and how much we've accomplished—but it has the opposite effect on the rest of the world. We "read" for them as being insecure, overwhelmed, uncomfortable in our job, and our own skin.

What can you do instead? Breathe. Smile. Slow down. Take the extra second or two to say good morning to your colleagues, end a phone call gracefully, comment on last night's televised sporting event. All of these things truly take only seconds away from the work you are doing, but they pay back big. The people around you are left with the impression of someone calm and in command.

## "Action!"

"What limits people is that they don't have the f\*\*\*ing nerve or imagination to star in their own movie, let alone direct it."

I ran into the above quote in Tom Robbins's *Still Life with Woodpecker* at a formative moment in my life—or what felt like a formative moment at the time. What I didn't realize then, but know beyond a shadow of a doubt now, is that thinking about every moment as potentially formative is what makes it so.

Here's what I mean by this. One day I was talking to a movie producer—asking him about his role in that work. Yes, he agreed, he did raise money. The main thing he did, however, was to think like a musical conductor: How was he going to get every member of his cast and crew to work at capacity from the starting note to the final chords, and in such a way as to make the work of the composer appear flawless?

Why was this important? Because a producer or director doesn't have the luxury of having an audience say to themselves, "Oh well, it's okay that that scene was a bit flat. . . . They probably shot it the first day." Or, "Oh well, it's okay that that part looks a bit out of focus; they must have been really tired shooting so many night scenes." No. The audience expects the movie to have a consistent brilliance from the get-go. Given that, everybody involved had to hit the ground running from the first moment the director said "Action!" on the first day.

How did he continuously inspire those around him to give their best?

It began with something so seemingly small that its importance is often overlooked. He learned the names and individual functions of each and every one of the one hundred members of the crew. This personalization of, and gratitude for, the individual contributions of each person went a long way toward earning their willingness to go the extra mile when situations demanded it.

Second, he impressed on each person present his own belief that, as Benjamin Franklin reminded us, "For the want of a nail, the shoe was lost; for the want of a shoe, the horse was lost; for the want of a horse the rider was lost," etc. In other words, regardless of the situation, it's the small details well and timely delivered that determine the outcome.

Finally, he felt it was critical to—as the seven dwarves remind us—whistle a happy tune. If those at the top appear to be relaxed and enjoying themselves, then everyone around will join in that energy, which produces enthusiasm, creativity, and commitment.

So, as you begin to direct and star in the movie of you, remember:

- No one is unimportant.
- No detail is small.
- No one wants a leader who appears anxious, upset, or uncertain. Whether you're a conductor, director, or parent, your team takes their cues from you.

## SUMMING IT UP:

- Remember that 7 percent of your impact comes from the words you say, 38 percent from your tonal quality while saying it, and 55 percent from what your body is doing while you're saying it.

- Speaking in story will help both you and your listener retain and commit to your message.

- Introducing yourself—saying your name—is a presentation opportunity. Don't squander it.

- Delete useless modifiers from your vocabulary. Something is only amazing, terrific, or horrific if you tell me *why*.

- Breathing from your diaphragm lowers your voice, increasing others' perception of your authority/command of your material and calming your nervous system.

- Make sure your words and tone match. If you're saying you're happy, you need to sound happy. If you're saying you're sorry, you need to sound sorry.

- "You" has been flagged as the most persuasive word in the English language. Use it often.

- When in doubt, wear blue. Investing in high-quality basics—a well-made suit, briefcase, or watch—will always pay off.

- Relaxing the back of your neck will help to calm the nerves controlling your digestion and respiration.

- Listen to find out, to discover, to explore.

- Writing a "Diary Entry for Tomorrow" can help you stay focused today.

- More isn't better. Better is better.

- When you give your listeners the "because" behind your decision, you increase buy-in from 60 to 94 percent.

- How you enter and exit a situation or conversation is as important as what occurs during that situation or conversation.

- If you only have Plan A and Plan B, then you don't actually have two options. Put together Plan C.

- Making the difficult look easy is far more impressive than "showing your work."

- Be sure you are the one directing and starring in your life.

## CHAPTER TWO

# Make It More Than "Just Lunch":
## The Art of the One-on-One Encounter

One-on-one. Regardless of the circumstances, there's an intimacy and immediacy to this type of encounter that often makes it the "extreme sports" version of presenting the self. Whether it's a handshake signaling a peace accord, a lunch where you're sealing a deal, or a basketball court where you're facing off against your toughest neighborhood competitor, one-on-one has an emotionality that makes our hearts beat faster.

Another reason the one-on-one encounter gets a section of its own is that for most of us life is a series of one-on-one encounters—we aren't speaking to crowds on a day-to-day basis. Instead, we're negotiating with our landlords, strategizing with our bosses, teaching our kids, thanking our neighbors, cultivating our coworkers, commiserating with our spouses, entertaining our friends, fundraising for our schools, tap-dancing on a shag rug for our in-laws . . .

Given that, the following tools are designed to help you read your listener more accurately, and so, choose the phrasing, physicality, and tonality he or she is most likely to respond to; also included are ways to help draw him or her out, to bring out the best in them, to make them feel acknowledged, comfortable, and confident. And who doesn't like someone who makes you feel like that?

Of course, since we are supposed to put on our own oxygen masks before we help those around us, I've also included tools you can use to increase your confidence—to reassure you that you do indeed have all that you need to shine in these moments.

## Visual, Aural, or Kinesthetic?

There are many different ways we take in information. We see, smell, taste, touch, and hear. Individually, however, we each have a primary intake pathway. Those who are more visual learn best through their eyes; those who are more auditory learn best through their ears; those who are more kinesthetic learn best through their bodies.

Knowing which you are can be very helpful. As an aural, I know that I learn best by listening—that taking notes while someone is talking can be distracting to me. Knowing that, it used to make me crazy when clients would take notes while I was talking. How could they take notes *and* listen? They obviously *weren't* listening, so I'd make them put down their pens and look at me—which, FYI, makes a kinesthetic stop listening.

Yes, kinesthetic types "listen" through their bodies—by writing down what you say. And no, it doesn't matter if neither you nor they can read their notes afterward. As nutty as it may seem to an aural or visual, it does help them listen. Visual types, on the other hand, don't seem like they are listening at all. They're the ones who are constantly interrupting, changing the subject, veering off on tangents. Why? Because our eyes take in thousands of impressions in seconds, so their words fly out, feeling like thousands in seconds.

How can you diagnose yourself? It's often pretty straightforward. By now, I imagine most of you have a pretty good idea of what you might be. If you're hovering between two choices, however, consider what you do for a living. Most of you will have made choices based on your primary intake pathway. For example, as an aural, I'm a word person. Talking and listening is my idea of fun. (Going to conferences and hearing people speak is my idea of courtside tickets to the Knicks.) My friend Jill is kinesthetic. She makes her living as an architect—which is all about spatial relations. I can't even pick out the right sized pan to pour a box of soup into. (Yes, it's true, I can't cook either.) My spatial relations reasoning is bad enough that I made Jill come with me to get a dog because I wasn't sure if what I was seeing as a small dog was, in fact, a small dog. My friends who are fashion designers and art dealers are visuals. They live through their eyes. Not me. Whenever we are together—whether it's at a gallery opening or a shoe sale—I'm constantly asking them, "Okay, am I having a taste lapse or is that beautiful?"

How can this help you in a one-on-one encounter? When you know someone's primary intake pathway, it helps in a number of ways. As I mentioned earlier, it can help you refrain from being impatient with the way they listen. Once I'd realized my kinesthetics needed their pens, I let them keep them. They also, often, need to walk around in meetings. So be it. You can do the same. Once I'd realized my visuals need to zoom off on tangents, I let them. Then I herd them back to the point . . . like getting a cat in a bag.

Here are some other benefits: realizing that much of the way someone is listening has little or nothing to do with how interesting you or your subject may or may not be, will help to keep you from taking it personally if they don't seem to be paying attention to you. In fact you'll realize that more often than not, they are. Additionally, it can help you to tailor how you give them information. If you're speaking to an aural, you can tell them you hear what they're saying. If you're speaking to a visual, you see what they're saying. If you're talking to a kinesthetic, you understand what they're feeling.

And, because you know this, it'll all be true.

## Read Between the Signs

As I'll get to in the "Meetings" chapter, how and where you sit is always important. In this essay, however, we're going to get into how your pitch target, or lunch date, is sitting, and how reading this, and responding to it, can lead to an entirely different conversation.

I used to go to pitch meetings with a partner who had a lot of trouble with this. In the interest of making his point, he would often lean in too closely while—well, browbeating isn't too strong a word—a listener. He would also interrupt others mid-sentence. His passion for making his point meant that he didn't see slumped shoulders as anything other than bad posture, averted gazes as anything other than bad manners. Drumming fingers, tapping feet . . . all the signs of "Here's your hat, what's your hurry?" were lost on him. He didn't read the signs. I remember one particularly hideously uncomfortable business dinner where the person whom we were there to woo and win over kept slumping farther and farther down on his spine, crossing and recrossing his arms across his chest, turning his chair, inch by inch, away from my partner, gazing fascinated at the restaurant's lighting fixtures. . . . Suffice to say, that deal died on the vine.

Now I'm not saying I've never gotten off at a wrong exit, but over time I've gotten pretty good at being able to hear what people are saying without their saying a word, and you can, too. And once you can, you can modify how you're speaking, what you're saying, and what your body is doing while you are saying it, so that others are more comfortable with you. You will leave your listeners feeling understood and energized.

What signs should you look for? As I mentioned earlier, gaze and posture are gigantic indicators of how your message is being received. If someone's gaze is averted initially, it may be that he or she is shy or uncomfortable. If, however, you are halfway through a lunch or a meeting and someone is no longer looking you in the eye, you need to take a moment and regroup. Ask yourself, "Could I have said something to embarrass? Offend? Distress?" After this, perhaps, do a delicate probe.

Why delicate? Because a question along the lines of, "You seem embarrassed/offended/distressed. Why?" makes it sound as if the conversation breakdown is the other person's fault. In these moments, it's more effective to take the onus on yourself: "Is there something I've said that isn't working for you?" "Is there a question you have that I haven't addressed?" etc, will help them to respond to you more easily.

Let me give you an example from a meeting situation. I was called in to work with a group of guys on a PowerPoint presentation they were preparing for potential investors. Since I never begin by talking, but by listening, I asked them to give me the presentation while I observed. When they finished, I gave them notes on this and that. Among these, I asked, "What's up with slide twelve? There seems to be some discomfort with it." Why did this question work? Because it was about the slide—it sounded like it was the *slide* that made me ask the question, not their twirling thumbs, or nervous pen-clicking, or averted gazes when it was on the screen. They were astonished, but relieved. There was, in fact, a gigantic issue with the slide. It seems they weren't going to be able to deliver on what it promised. Suffice to say, we clarified the text to reflect this truth before we continued.

As you begin to recognize these signs of feeling nervous, defeated, or misunderstood, and ask questions in ways that allow your listeners to comfortably express their opinions, display their strengths, and demonstrate their expertise, they will blossom. Requesting their contribution in this way will also help you enhance your contribution.

## Every Villain Is the Hero of His Own Story

The above is a line I heard Mike Myers use in his *Inside the Actors Studio* interview. Yes, he was talking about Dr. Evil, but I believe this idea can be applied anytime you are dreading a one-on-one with someone because their values, ethics, or interests are at odds with your own.

For example, perhaps you know your lunch date is someone who adores golf. His idea of heaven is eighteen holes at his country club on a sunny Saturday. Aside from the fact that hearing people talk about golf makes you want to take a nap, you find the idea of private country clubs abhorrent, elitist, etc.

What to do?

I would ask you to do more than avoid the subject during lunch. I would ask you to put yourself in his shoes before you get there. To perhaps consider a sport about which you are passionate—baseball for example—and imagine how you might feel if your lunch date pointed out that anyone who thought that standing around in the grass with a gigantic leather oven mitt on his hand could be called playing a sport was ridiculous. It's possible you might be a little miffed by this. It's possible you might think your lunch date was a wanker. If he were to go on to say that anyone who found sitting in a stadium where you can't see the game while drinking beer and eating a hot dog a pleasurable afternoon should have their head examined, you might get actively offended.

If you're thinking there's no comparison—that baseball is, after all, as American as apple pie—it's time to make them the hero of their own story. To ask yourself why they might care so much about golf or the club. To consider factors like, "Maybe he was a terrible athlete in high school, and golf is something he's discovered he's good at." Or, "Maybe he was teased for not belonging to the local club as a child, so he places enormous value on belonging."

The purpose of this exercise is not to sway you in your own views, but to help you listen to your arguments with new ears, to consider what factors might be in play that might be unspoken. Is it possible the "shop window" they are presenting has a lot behind it that might be influencing their presentation in ways you can't see at first glance? Depending on the scenario, could they have family concerns or health concerns or financial concerns you're unaware of?

Asking yourself these kinds of questions can expose holes or gaps in your knowledge that can then be strengthened through in-depth conversation. As it becomes obvious to them that you have taken the time to research and try to understand their position, it will be far easier for them to hear and possibly understand yours.

## What's Their Egg?

The above is a question I ask my clients a lot. It comes from what I refer to as The Duncan Hines Cake Mix Marketing Theory.

Here's how the story goes: when Duncan Hines was first putting together their cake mix the decision was made *in the marketing department* to have the at-home "cook" add an egg to the mix, rather than putting powdered egg in the mix themselves. Why? Because when we add the egg, we take ownership of the cake. We are proud. We feel okay saying, "I baked!" Making us feel better about buying a mix makes us buy a mix more often.

Smart, right?

Actively courting others' participation in this way is vitally important when you want support for your idea, money for your project, votes for your ballot box . . . any kind of buy-in.

How can you do this?

Before your meeting, ask yourself: "Why is this person's unique contribution valuable to me and to the project?"

Why is it important that you articulate what *they alone* can bring to the party? Because we all want to believe our contributions are valuable, that we are necessary, that we can make a difference, that we are more than a blank check or a hand on a lever.

Having discovered this—and with the right amount of preparation it can be discovered—frame any request you are making in such a way that it will be easy for them to "add the egg": to contribute to your idea.

Let me give you an example. I have a good friend who's an actor. She was going in to meet with a producer about a movie role she wanted *a lot*, so she called me to strategize. First, I asked her about the part. It was the role of a very strong-minded woman—an iconic character. Then, I asked her what other films this producer had made. His roster was long, and it happened to include two films with female leads that are universally recognized to have permanently changed perceptions of the roles of women in our society. This was his egg! His gift was being unafraid to bring strong women to the screen, and creating a safe space for actors to portray these risky roles.

Armed with this knowledge my friend was able to go into the meeting better prepared than any of her competitors. She was able to say, "There aren't a lot of men in the world who would take on this story—this female character—even if she is fictional! But knowing your work on X and Y, it came as no surprise to me that you were un-daunted by her. I'm certain you'll create a similarly groundbreaking character this time out, and I'd like to hear how you're thinking about doing it. Then, I'd like to tell you what I will contribute . . ."

You see? Articulating both what, and how important, his unique contribution was going to be—rather than simply stating what hers would be—made it easier for him to say, "I baked!" Finding his egg in advance of the meeting was the respect she paid him, which made it easier for him to hear her.

People want to contribute. Finding their egg is how you can help them do that. So, the next time you are getting ready to make a big request of another—whether it's financial or emotional, business or personal—take the time to ask, and answer, the question: "What's their egg?"

## Your Black Book for Lunch

Whether you are the host or the guest at a lunch, advance reconnais-sance is necessary. As always, it's never "just lunch." Despite what the dating service may say, both host and guest need to do their home-work once a lunch date has been agreed upon. If you are the host, be aware that your prep work will need to be more in-depth.

*As the host:* If you are unfamiliar with the restaurant, you will want to scout it out in person ahead of time, if possible, to check the noise level and decide which table best suits your purpose. This is important because, if it's a business lunch, you don't want to find yourself sitting knee-to-knee at a corner table with your guest, being lulled by contempo-pop or trying to make yourself heard over hip hop. I'm also particular about tables that are too close together, i.e., I don't like it. I need room for scope. I don't want to feel like the person next to me is going to ask for a bite of something off my plate.

If you can't arrange to do an on-site check ahead of time, arrange to get there fifteen minutes early to triage any elements you can—get yourself moved to a different table, a quieter area, ask to have the music turned down, etc.

You will want to have gotten the name of the manager or staff person who will be responsible for ensuring things run smoothly and, if possible, introduced yourself to him or her.

You will want to know where the bathrooms are located.

You will want to have inquired whether there are vegetarian options on the menu, should your guest be vegetarian. (FYI: Chicken and fish are not vegetables.) If there is nothing immediately apparent, ask if a vegetarian option can be prepared if necessary. It generally can.

You will want to have made sure they take your credit card. Some places don't take American Express. Some places only take American Express.

*As the guest:* You will want to research the restaurant online before you arrive. In addition to confirming the address, if it's a restaurant that's unknown to you, you will want to check whether parking is readily available nearby, or if you will need to allow time to look for a space or possibly walk a few minutes from your car to the restaurant.

You will want to be on time.

You will want to have allowed time to use the bathroom prior to your scheduled meeting time, if that's necessary. (I know it seems mad that I have to write this down, but I can't tell you how many people arrive at lunch meetings and leave me at the table for the first ten minutes while they go to the bathroom.)

You will want to follow your host's lead regarding whether or not he or she wants to dive right into a business conversation. I prefer to allow a bit of time before getting into "why we're here today." You will, of course, have done advance prep on your host's interests/

hobbies so this small talk time will be meaningful. If that hasn't been possible, and the answer isn't immediately apparent—e.g., it's the only game in town, or it has a five-star reputation—ask why your host chose the restaurant. Is it a favorite? Is there something he or she would recommend? Have they taken trips to its country of origin? (Italy, France, Greece, Turkey, Brazil . . . ? You get the idea.)

If there is anything funky about your place setting or your food, short of visible shards of broken glass or the possibility of anaphylactic shock, you will want to keep it to yourself. It's not the time to comment on smears on your knife, or your feelings about the unexpected use of balsamic vinegar in your salad. If there is something that needs to be addressed, ask your host to handle it with the restaurant. It's not your job.

You will want to enjoy yourself. The greatest compliment you can pay your host is to be attentive, relaxed, and appreciative.

## Manners Maketh Man

I flip-flopped a lot about writing this particular section as the status attached to "good manners" was so overblown in my house when I was growing up that I've been leery of imposing them on others ever since. And if you think I'm joking you can call my poor sister who was sent from the table, in tears, for eating her toast incorrectly.

That said, there are certain fundamental manners that will smooth the way in social situations. I'll move through them quickly here, but feel free to pick up *Tiffany's Table Manners for Teenagers* if you want a quick, in-and-out hit, or Emily Post or Amy Vanderbilt if you want to go deeper.

If you arrive at the restaurant before your lunch partner, you may choose to wait for him or her at the bar or at the table. In general, I wait at the table, but this is often a judgment call based on your relationship with the person you are meeting, and the space you're meeting in. If you know the person well, or the bar is set up to facilitate the waiting process, the bar can be a fine choice. Should you choose to go to the table, feel free to order the water or soft drink of your choice. You will not be having an alcoholic drink.

If you arrive at the restaurant with your lunch partner, and you are a party of one man and one woman, the man should stand back and let the woman follow the maître d' to the table—even if he made the reservation. If you are two men, let your guest go first. This ensures your guest will get the best seat at the table. If you are the woman, and the host, you can give your male lunch partner the better seat on his arrival. That said, I do make exceptions for people with extremely long legs. Notice if someone has them. If so, put him or her where there's the most room.

Your napkin goes in your lap immediately after sitting down.

If you are offered a roll, break it in pieces and butter each piece individually just before eating it. Do not cut it in half and butter it like a sandwich.

Check in with your host about what he or she might be ordering. If it's just an entrée, follow that lead. You don't want to be tucking into a foie gras appetizer followed by a whole, deboned fish if all your host ordered is a salad.

Please do not discuss your feelings about carbohydrates, white flour, white sugar, eating fats, the use of bovine growth hormone, the conditions under which chickens are raised, or your latest diet plan, should you be on one. If you are lactose intolerant, wheat intolerant, or have too much candida, keep it to yourself. If you are a vegetarian, pescetarian, vegan, fruitarian, raw foodist, don't bring it up unless directly asked. If you are asked, respond and move on. Unless your eating plan is the focus of the meal, this is not the time or place to discuss those habits.

Order food that's easy to manage. For example, if you have the choice between vegetable or onion soup, order the vegetable soup. No one wants to see you playing cat's cradle with the cheese on top of the onion soup. If you have a choice between a green salad and a frisee salad, get the green salad. No one wants to see the frisee hanging out of your mouth like calamari legs. If you have the choice between pasta and ravioli, choose the ravioli, etc, etc.

Don't forget to use "please" and "thank you" with the waitstaff as they take your order and bring your food.

For multiple courses, choose the fork or spoon farthest from your plate for your first course and work your way inward.

Please hold your fork like a pencil, not like a trowel. I can't say this emphatically enough. It is one place my mother lives in me. Yes, it means you will have to transfer your fork to your dominant hand if you are using both your fork and knife. This modicum of effort is worth the payoff.

Sit up straight.

Should you need to go to the bathroom, excuse yourself to use the ladies' or men's room. You aren't going to the john, the restroom, or the powder room. You are definitely not going to "hit the head." Leave your napkin on your chair when you go, not on the table.

If you are asked if you want coffee at the end of the meal, again, follow your host's lead. If he or she declines coffee, you should too. Know that some people think ordering cappuccino after 11 A.M. is infamous. I'm not saying I buy into that particular brand of thinking, I'm just making you aware that it exists.

Your host will handle the bill. Do not feel the need to chatter as he or she does so.

A simple "Thank you so much for a lovely lunch" will suffice, since you will be following up with a handwritten thank-you note.

## Oh, Those Windows of the Soul

It's possible this essay may be one where a few of you start thinking it's time to get off the *How to Wow* party train. That it's been fun, but we are now headed into territory so peculiar, so uncharted by science or Western medicine, that it's obvious I've exchanged my conductor's hat for a jester's.

Stay with me.

Here's the thing, I've spent a lot of time studying Ayurvedic—Indian—medicine. Not a lot of time by their standards, where a degree takes twelve years of medical school to get, but a lot of time by Western standards. Given that, I've obviously bought into its broad concepts. That said, I'm not asking you to. I'm simply giving you this information as I've found it's true, and effective. Whether you choose to believe it, or simply make use of it, or ultimately discard it, is up to you. I'm simply handing out refreshments on the train.

Okay, so Ayurvedic medicine states that the right side of your body is governed by fire, the left side of your body is governed by water. The right is about deciding, commanding, defending. The left is about receiving, accepting, surrendering. If you're willing to accept that, consider that your eyes could be a place where these two aspects of fire and water are visible.

Now, if you're really interested—or skeptical—go to a mirror and look into your left eye. Feel what comes up when you do. Then switch, and look into your right eye and notice what you feel when you do. It's possible you'll find that your left eye is warmer, more inviting, while your right tends to be challenging.

"Okay," you're thinking, "so I did the exercise." (Or you didn't.) "What am I supposed to do with the information?"

Well, now that you know it, it could be that the next time you really want to convey to another person that your intention and your message is genuine, trustworthy, sincere, etc . . . you could make a point of looking into their left eye while you do this. If you were to do that, it's possible they would accept what you were saying more readily. If you wanted to issue a challenge, or convey that what you were saying was not negotiable, you might look into their right eye when you said it. It's entirely up to you, but I'm guessing they would realize more quickly that their compliance was mandatory.

Do with this information what you will. My point is that there's no downside to checking it out. You don't need to announce it (or heaven forbid, put it in your book); you can simply, literally, see what happens.

## The Eyes Have It

By now we're all pretty familiar with the concept of the eyes as the windows of the soul—or at the very least we've been told a few dozen times that eye contact is important for communicating our message. The following facts did a lot to reinforce this idea for me, so I thought I'd share them with you:

- Did you know that the number one poker "tell"—a habit, behavior, or physical reaction that gives away information about your hand—is to give away your hand by staring too long at big hole cards or fail to look your fellow players in the eyes when they ask if you've got a good hand (few of us can look others in the eyes when we're being dishonest)? This is why most professional poker players wear sunglasses or hats with visors.

- Did you know that the OPEC negotiators wear sunglasses during those negotiations?

- Did you know that the purpose of secret service officers wearing sunglasses is less about protection from glare and more about making potential attackers uneasy about whether or not they have been singled out for surveillance?

# He Listened/She Listened

A few years ago I attended a communication seminar run by an extraordinary woman named Alison Armstrong. The focus of Alison's work has been to pinpoint and clarify the profound differences in the way men and women communicate. The point she makes is that the communication choices each sex makes aren't voluntary, they're due to the way we're wired; neither way is better or worse, they're simply very, very different. And in the same way you aren't going to have a lot of success using the television remote to try to work the toaster, you aren't going to have a lot of success communicating with the opposite sex if you don't have the correct tools for the job. Given that, here are a few of her tools:

Men are single-focus. This can be demonstrated in multiple

ways, but the easiest is to point out that this is often why they don't enjoy shopping. For example, if you ask them to come with you to look for a white shirt and they look over and see you trying on a pair of shoes, they can get cranky. Why are you trying on shoes when you said you're looking for a white shirt? The fact that they are perfect summer slingbacks marked down to next-to-nothing means nothing to them. Shoes were not on the itinerary when they signed on for the expedition.

A by-product of this single focus is that they have two default listening modes: What's the point? Or, what's the problem? This is not to say that they can't listen in other ways, but these are their go-to styles. Consequently, it's vitally important for women to stay "on task" when speaking with the men in their lives. If you're a woman and the thrust of your message to your male colleague is that the report's not ready, don't clutter that up with why unless the why is something he can fix. If it's simply due to random internal glitches your male colleague will generally stop listening, or cut you off, if you begin to specify them. This is not because he doesn't care, but because those "whys" aren't vital information.

The flip side of this, of course, is when your story has a point, but requires a somewhat longer lead. On these occasions, I've found it helpful to include something along the lines of, "It may sound like this is off subject/irrelevant, but it's critical to the point I'm going to be making in a moment," at the outset.

Women, on the other hand, have diffuse awareness, which is why we can answer the phone, put the dog outside, make a snack for our child, and drink tea simultaneously. It's the reason those slingbacks caught our eye in the first place. In a work scenario, this translates into our having a higher threshold of tolerance for taking in multiple thoughts or details, both relevant and seemingly irrelevant. In fact, we do more than take them in, we like them. They allow us to add to and perfect our personal "central intelligence" network. It's one of the reasons we will often interrupt with clarifying questions or requests for additional detail. In these instances, it's important for our male colleagues not to feel we aren't paying attention, or that we're being rude. We simply have a different default listening setting.

So the next time you find yourself frustrated by your male colleague's inattention, or your female colleague's interruptions, take a moment to check your default listening setting, and then, tune in to their frequency.

## State the Obvious

Ironically, this idea is so often overlooked that it almost didn't make it into the book. Perhaps because it forces us to look at a very human aspect of our human nature. Perhaps because we're unsure that it's appropriate. Perhaps because it seems so obvious that it didn't seem to need its own essay . . . but perhaps this is exactly why it does. Here it is: Sometimes, it's important to state the obvious.

Let me give you an example of what I mean by this. One of my clients is handsome. Very, very handsome. So handsome that it's one of the first things most people comment on when they talk about him. The thing is, though, that people rarely say it to him.

Now this happens for a number of reasons. Partly, of course, because it isn't something that is appropriate to bring up in most conversations. Sometimes, however, it's because people assume he knows it; sometimes because people are still adhering to the idea of not feeding into someone's "swelled head"; sometimes, simply, because people are jealous. So, for any number of reasons, no one ever says it to him.

It came up for us when we were talking about a strategy for presenting a controversial campaign and I listed his looks as one of his assets. His reaction? He was surprised, embarrassed, pleased, and—in a way—relieved. It was the elephant in the room and someone had finally spoken about it. My willingness to talk about it frankly and objectively made it something he could feel comfortable with, rather than embarrassed by or ashamed of. This mental shift went a long way toward helping him come across as comfortable in his own skin.

What are other examples of this kind? Perhaps someone has a

beautiful corner office, but no one ever admires the view because they assume he or she knows it. I don't doubt they do, but it can be nice to have someone else appreciate it, too. Perhaps someone has honor roll kids, or a stunning piece of jewelry or a brand-new sports car. Whatever it might be, if it's being talked about during the water cooler gossip, or in your after-work conversations with your spouse, I'm willing to bet no one ever speaks about how terrific or beautiful it is to them. And this can be nice to hear.

The same can be true about negative things. Sometimes I get called in to talk to people about a negative "obvious" that—because it's so obvious—no one wants to get into. Someone sweats a lot during presentations, or their clothes are too tight, or they have a habit of rolling their eyes up into their head when they are thinking. . . . Whatever it might be, no one wants to mention it, either because they assume he or she *must* know it, because it makes them uncomfortable, or because they're fearful of the long-term repercussions of tackling it themselves.

The thing is, though, that very often even if the person in question does suspect or know it, the fact that no one is talking about it has made it so overwhelming to them that they can't begin to ask for help or advice. In these moments, having another person say, "I've noticed this. Have you?" can feel like having someone open a window into a dark, stuffy room. It lets enough air into the conversation for everyone to relax and breathe and tackle the issue objectively.

So the next time you find yourself thinking, "Well, he or she must *know* that. It's so obvious!" consider taking the time to articulate whatever that might be to them. Whether it's positive or negative, you might be surprised at the pleasure or relief in their response.

## When Softer Is Stronger

I was writing earlier about poker tells, the habits, behaviors, or physical reactions that give away your hand to others at the poker table.

One of the ones I found most interesting, though not most surprising, was weak is strong/strong is weak. It seems that the tendency to look disinterested when you have a great hand is something more generally practiced by novice players, but some experienced poker-types fall into it as well.

Victor Hugo, the French poet and novelist best known for fictionalizing his social commentary in *Les Miserables,* said much the same thing about giveaways in language: "Strong and bitter words indicate a weak cause."

A variant of this idea—that a show of force isn't indicative of your chances of winning your round, making your point, or getting your way—was also endorsed by former president Theodore Roosevelt who brought the West African proverb, "Speak softly but carry a big stick. You will go far," into popular consciousness.

I buy into it too. Over and over again I have noticed that those who are most into "show" and "tell" are generally overcompensating for weakness in their argument, their financials, their self-esteem. When this occurs, I've found that greeting these displays with softness, acceptance, and compassion is a far faster way to gain their trust and arrive at their truth than trying to match them with your own show and tell.

Here are two examples from my experience:

One of the first people with whom I worked walked into the room and, before introducing himself, said, "Here is a list of the things I will not discuss with the press: X, Y, Z."

I said, "Okay."

He said, "It simply won't happen."

I said, "I understand."

This choice was surprising enough to him for him to want to explain himself to me—not the subjects that were off limits, but his reasoning for putting them off limits. The opportunity to speak his piece defused an enormous amount of his tension. It also gave me the chance to understand and acknowledge the validity of his concerns. Once this very human connection was established we were able to move quickly through the taboo subjects, collaborating on ways to speak about them that were both revealing to the press yet comfortable for him.

In another instance a client called me for advice on dealing with two colleagues who had spent the better part of six months jerking him around about whether or not he would be the one to lead an agency project. Though the idea of responding in kind was tempting, he had a sense it would only escalate the madness. I agreed. Together we worked through a strategy for handling the ongoing negotiation—everything must be put in writing, everyone must be cc'd on every piece of correspondence pertaining to the deal—and a way of talking to them about that choice, "In order to short-circuit future misunderstandings I'm instituting the following policy," etc. Notice please, there were no statements along the lines of, "Because you told me one thing on Monday and another on Tuesday, I've been forced to institute the following policy . . ."

The consequence of this was that the other players no longer had the opportunity to pass the buck or backpedal on earlier statements. If and when they tried to, my client was able to be very factual in his response, "On X date you promised Y." With nowhere to run and nowhere to hide, they folded and gave him the project. And because he'd handled the negotiation "bloodlessly"—without raising his voice or falling back on "you" statements along the lines of, "But you said you would do X," their resentment level for being called out stayed low, which made working on the project with them far more bearable.

## Channel Your Inner Clooney or Kelly

One of the television shows I love most is Bravo's *Inside the Actors Studio*. This weekly hour-long, in-depth conversation between the host, James Lipton, and a guest actor, is endlessly fascinating to me. I love to hear how different people approach their lives and their work.

Among the best interviews I think I've seen (which is saying something when you consider the caliber of the guests) was with Johnny Depp—and not just because I find him utterly, heart-stoppingly gorgeous. It was because of the way he described how he prepares for his films.

For example, when he was asked about *Edward Scissorhands*, he said his goal had been to combine the innocence of a newborn baby with that quality in a dog that allows him to be reprimanded and sent to his crate one minute, and yet come bounding out with a heart full of love when he was next called. When he was asked about his role in *Ed Wood*, he said he wanted to combine the blind optimism of Ronald Reagan with the overt geniality of Casey Kasem. For *Pirates of the Caribbean*, he looked to the Rolling Stones's Keith Richards as a role model.

In every case, the minute he said it, I got it. It was, in fact, exactly what he had done.

How can this help you? What I've found with my clients is that this idea of embodying the qualities of someone they admire can be very helpful to them as they begin to find their footing in a challenging speaking situation. In the same way it's often easier to solve our friends' problems than it is to solve our own, it's often easier to imagine how someone you see as confident, or suave, or independent might tackle your life.

For this reason, two of the questions I ask every client in their pre-session questionnaire are, "Who do you admire as a communicator/ presenter?" and "Why do you admire him or her?" Then, if he or she runs into a stumbling block later, I can say, "Okay how would Bill Clinton, (or Diane Sawyer, or Jon Stewart, or Oprah, or your boss— which comes up more frequently than you might imagine) handle this? What would they say or do?" Rethinking it from that point of view is often exactly what they need to find the confidence to carry the day.

So whatever role you may be preparing for, it's often helpful to say to yourself, "I need to be sassy, but elegant. . . . I'm thinking, Erin Brockovich meets Grace Kelly," "I need to be commanding and inspiring. . . . Winston Churchill meets Mother Teresa," or "I need to be charismatic but accessible. . . . George Clooney meets Jimmy Stewart."

And, in addition to being helpful, it can actually be fun.

## "Go up. Don't come down."

Of course, with all of this thinking and planning and practicing it's possible that, like Charlie Brown with his book report, you can stall yourself out completely—get so far up in your head with the technical aspects of what needs to get done that you forget the basic premise from which you began, the reason behind why you are speaking in the first place. Suddenly you discover that what began as a manageable project has begun spiraling downward into a mass of directions and complications and contradictions.

When this happens for me, I like to remember what my yoga teacher said when a student asked him about doing headstands. The student had a dozen questions: should he be putting his hands this way? his head there? his elbows closer together? further apart??

My teacher said, "Go up. Don't come down."

A man of few words.

During his *Inside the Actors Studio* interview, I heard Matt Damon tell a similar story about being directed by the Farrelly brothers during their film *Stuck on You*. Apparently Damon and Greg Kinnear were waiting and waiting for their director's notes. What Bobby Farrelly finally said to them was, "Okay . . . suck less."

Sometimes it really is that simple.

So the next time you find yourself feeling anxious, or overwhelmed by the advice of friends, family, coworkers, take a moment and see if you can break it down to the most basic direction possible. What you may discover is that making things easier for yourself will make it easier for those around you, which will make it easier for you . . . .

At which point you'll discover that instead of spiraling down, you're now spiraling up.

## "I was just joking!" Um . . . No

It's possible that after reading this essay you might decide I'm not a lot of fun to have in the office down the hall, or at your holiday party. You might be right . . . or it might just be that I'm fun *in a different kind of way*.

So here it is. I tend to listen very carefully to what other people are saying all the time. I tend to point like a gundog when I hear the phrase, "Oh, I was just joking."

Why? Because I find that that particular verbal tic usually flags a moment when a person isn't joking at all. When they are using humor either to say something they're uncomfortable about saying, or are unaware they feel strongly about. Wrapping these uncomfortable or strong feelings in humor is a way of protecting themselves while they test-drive others' reactions. Will their listener respond in kind? Will he get offended?

If a person responds in kind, the usual next step is mutual delight in their ostensibly shared "sense of humor"; this generally quickly degenerates into a wholesale bitch session about whatever they claimed to find so funny just moments before. If their listener gets offended, a quick exit generally follows: to anything from a pressing call, to an urgent appointment, to a fresh drink.

The same is often true if you listen closely to what people joke about without their flagging it with "I was just joking." If you find someone's telling a lot of "funny" stories about fights with their spouse or being able to make their next car payment, it's more than likely a divorce or the liquidation of some of their assets is in the not-too-distant future.

So what can you do if it's something you need to tackle head-on, not just something you notice in the conference room or at a cocktail party? My first piece of advice is: Don't make any sudden moves—don't point out that you've heard people often joke about their true feelings, "So *what is it exactly that you're trying to say??*" This ends badly. As your mother used to say when she saw the board game or pillow fight escalating toward hysteria, "This ends in tears."

Instead, to return to the dog analogy, you want to use your herding instincts to move the conversation out of humor and toward authenticity. You can do this by acknowledging the joke without playing into it—either by admitting you yourself have felt some of the feelings you think are behind their joke, or by asking leading questions along the lines of, "That's an interesting way to look at it. Can you tell me a little more about what you mean?" Or, "Wow, you seem to have noticed something I hadn't picked up on. Did something happen that made you think this, or is it just your intuition?"

Again, in these moments I advise proceeding with care. If these feelings are strong enough that the person's fallen back on humor to defuse or deny them, they're generally extremely strong feelings once the "ha ha" factor has been taken away. So, listen a lot. Don't jump to conclusions. Take John Wayne's advice: "Talk low, talk slow, and don't say too much."

## We Dislike Most in Others
## What We Don't Like in Ourselves

This is a phrase you hear a lot if you spend any time in a psychologist's office, or in the psychology section of the bookstore. I think it's valid, although it can be hard to hear. It is, after all, so much more satisfying (i.e., less scary) to note others' failings and shortcomings than to turn the mirror on ourselves—to point out how and why they should be doing things differently, rather than consider and put into practice the ways we could be doing things differently.

I'll give you an example from my own life. A few years ago I was talking with my career coach about a friend, and talking would be a nice way of putting it. In reality I was in the middle of a full-fledged tirade about how she was spoiled, self-indulgent, wasteful of her potential. "Okay," he said. "Maybe so. But could part of the reason you're so agitated be because you haven't left your job, even though you've been talking about leaving forever—telling me it isn't challenging enough? Is it possible she pisses you off so much because you're not working to your potential either?"

Ouch. Yes.

As they say, sometimes the truth hurts. And this is why this particular piece of wisdom isn't something I advise you to turn on others. It's quite easy for it to misfire if you do—either blow back on you or be used inappropriately by them.

For example, in the early stages of dating a new boyfriend I got a little cranky about some nitpicking he was doing about one of my possibly less-than-endearing traits, so I pointed out that when I found myself being really critical of someone else it was often because they reflected something I didn't like about myself; and that when I noticed that, I tried to look first at what I was bringing to the nutty, rather than pointing out my perception of their failings to them. His response to this was, "Well, aren't you just Little Miss Perfect."

Um . . . next!

Alternatively, I was once talking with a friend who was furious with a son who was lying to him and everyone else. Ever helpful, I pointed out that this might be behavior his kid had picked up close to home . . . from him, for example. Unfortunately, his response to that was to go blame his ex-wife for their son's facility with lying.

This did not end well. As noted, this is not a tool to use on others without some kind of professional qualification of your own.

That said, I continue to feel it's a powerful tool to use on ourselves. To take the time when we're really, really steamed about the way our coworker or boss or friend is behaving to ask ourselves, "Is there something in here that reflects my own fears or insecurities about myself?" The answer may not be pretty, but it will often be enlightening.

## "Hi, you've reached . . ."

These days, voice mail is ubiquitous. But like so many things in this category—mugs and baseball caps come immediately to my mind—

it's rare to come across a voice mail message that's really appealing, much less knocks your socks off.

Why is this important? Because your voice mail message is often the first contact a new person has with you. Consequently, it's an opportunity to impress someone right from the start. Despite this, however, I hear far, far too many voice mails that are less than memorable, and more than a few that do the person active disservice.

Here's an example:

One day I got a call from a client who had just promoted a mid-level manager to a top spot. I asked her if there was anything in particular I should be aware of. Well, she said, he's smart and enthusiastic—which is great—but we're worried he doesn't come across as "manager material."

Next, I called his office to make an appointment. Here's what his voice mail message sounded like:

"HI THIS IS JOE I'M NOT HERE LEAVE A MESSAGE OR CALL LEWIS AT 212 . . ."

Instead of sounding competent, calm, and in command, he sounded like he was trying to find his way out of a burning building.

Was it Joe's goal to come across this way? Of course not. It was simply that no one had ever told him how important this seemingly small detail was to the overall impression he left behind. Although we worked on a lot in his session, we began by rerecording his voice mail message. Now, should you call, you'll hear a message that's authoritative, warm, and welcoming—manager material, which he is.

So how should you go about recording your voice mail message?

- You want to record it while standing and smiling. This will give your voice warmth and energy. If you sound even slightly flat/tired/anxious/impatient/distracted/drunk/flirtatious or like you are speaking to children, redo it.
- You do not want any background or ambient noise. No cars, music, dogs barking, telephones ringing, etc.
- You want to inhale before you begin to record and speak on an exhalation as you begin to leave your message. This gives your

voice resonance and authority. *Note please* that you want to inhale *before* you begin to record. We don't want to hear you sucking in a big breath before you start speaking.

- You want to be sure that your name and any alternate numbers and—should you have one—your assistant's name and number are distinctly articulated. If you, or they, have an unusual name, you will want to speak even more slowly.

- You want to make sure it is current. Updating it should be the first thing you do on returning from a business trip or vacation. Among the many benefits of doing this is the fact that once it is done, you will always have that recording of you as your best self—even on days when you might, perhaps, not be.

---

### Mirror, Mirror . . .

Many of my clients do interviews on the telephone. Others work as salespeople, with the telephone as their tool. It goes without saying that since your interviewer or sales call can't see you, you lose an enormous amount of your potential to persuade. Consequently, the tone of your voice is extremely important: You need to sound authoritative, engaging, and extremely animated.

An easy way to ensure this is to look at yourself in a mirror as you talk. (Ideally, you will also be standing, which automatically gives your voice more animation.) The reason for this is that it's human instinct to interact with yourself when you see a mirror. You'll smile, you'll try to amuse yourself, you'll check to see how persuasive and engaging you look, and your voice will follow along—expressing the full range of its capabilities—automatically making you more interesting to the person listening to you.

---

## Making "Let's stay in touch" a Reality

Sometimes your one-on-one meeting goes *great*—so well that the last memory you have of your prospective client or business partner is their saying, "I'll be in touch," while gripping your right hand and beaming into your eyes. Thrilled, you go back to your office or your spouse and say, "I nailed it! I'm just waiting for the green light call . . . ." Only to find yourself sitting by the phone a week or two later with that sinking sensation you thought you'd left behind in high school.

Alternatively, sometimes you leave a meeting thinking, "Ugh. I blew it. I never hit my stride/There was no chemistry/I couldn't get a read on him/What *was* that??"

Both of these scenarios occur more frequently than you might think, and both are eminently salvageable if you orchestrate your follow-up as carefully as you did your meeting.

The first thing you need to do is to drop the temptation to take it personally. It's business, after all. The second thing you need to do is take it very personally—but from the point of view of the person in question. You need to ask yourself what possible roadblocks or set-backs or crises he might be experiencing; I don't want you to get wedded to any of your ideas, but I do want you to incorporate that mindset into your follow-up strategy. People go back to the office to find out their boss has been fired, their patent hasn't been approved, their kid's been arrested, their spouse is having an affair, their iden-tity's been stolen. Or they show up at their meeting with you having just discovered their boss has been fired, their patent hasn't been ap-proved, their kid's been arrested, their spouse is having an affair, their identity's been stolen. And any one of these scenarios is going to eat up the mental bandwidth necessary to forge a new connection. So, be kind—rewind. Approach your follow-up as mentally free of judg-ment as you can.

If X had said he would be calling you and a week to ten days have gone by with no contact, feel free to pick up the phone and leave a message for him, keeping it neutral both in language and in tone. Something along the lines of, "It was great to meet you. I wanted to follow up on our conversation about X, Y, Z. I can be reached by e-mail or phone," etc.

This particular phrasing works first because it reminds him of how well the meeting went. Second, it doesn't accuse him of any-thing; you haven't said, "I was expecting to hear from you by now/You said you were going to call by the end of last week," or some such. Instead, it's proactive: "I wanted to follow up." Third, including the X, Y, Z points discussed refreshes his memory on the details, which makes it easier for him to call you back; he doesn't have to scrabble back through his recollections or refer to his notes. And, finally, giving him the option to respond via phone or e-mail gives him the freedom to choose how he wants to get back to you in the way he feels most comfortable.

If this doesn't net you a reply, don't be afraid to try at least twice more, each time keeping your tone neutral and your language proactive and specific. If you still don't receive a response, I'd drop it. It's rare that someone you have to work that hard to connect with is going to be someone you want to work with on an ongoing basis.

If you do hear from him and there's been a business or personal glitch along the lines mentioned, sympathize but don't ask for details: "I'm sorry to hear that" suffices—note: *sound sorry*. Then ask when it would be best for you to be back in touch. Again, it's important to be proactive. Don't say, "Why don't you give me a call when things settle down?" because when they do, it's unlikely you and your deal are going to be at the top of the priority list. If it seems he went back to his office and rethought the whole thing, ask him for the details on his concerns. Don't bluster or try to change his mind. Let him speak his piece in full. When he's finished tell him you take his reservations seriously and are going to give them some thought. Once you have, if you still think there's a way to move forward, send him an e-mail outlining your ideas. Again, it's important not to judge his concerns, just to address them. If this doesn't turn it around, my best advice is to let it go. He will either come back around when he's had time to ruminate, or he won't. If he doesn't, again, it's unlikely it would have been a good fit after all.

If X left with no mention of following up but you're still interested in pursuing the connection, I suggest sending along an e-mail, or—more eye-catching still—a handwritten note, saying it was a pleasure to meet him (only you need to know that the pleasure in this instance was in the S & M family) and outlining the original reasons why you made the connection. It may be that this will arrive in a moment when he can focus on it in a way he wasn't able to during your one-on-one encounter, and he'll pick up the phone. Or it may be that his reservations will remain but your persistence will net you a second meeting; one for which you'll now know the X factor and so, can strategize accordingly.

## SUMMING IT UP:

- Knowing your, and your listener's, primary intake pathway—verbal, aural, or kinesthetic—and organizing yourself and your material accordingly will help increase both your and their retention and impact.

- Pay attention to others' gaze and posture. If one's averted and the other's defensive, you need to pause and regroup.

- If you're dreading a conversation because your values, ethics, or beliefs are at odds with theirs, try to imagine them as the hero of their own story.

- Find their "egg." What will they be contributing that's unique to them? Articulating this to them will increase the chances of their participation.

- Lunch is never "just lunch." Advance reconnaissance on both your companion's background and the restaurant where you'll be meeting is a must.

- Knowing and adhering to basic good manners is the equivalent of knowing and adhering to the rules of a sport: both are necessary for participants' safety and enjoyment.

- Looking into your listener's left eye while speaking to them increases their reception to, and acceptance of, your message.

- Men and women are wired for different listening styles—men are single-focus; women are diffuse-focus. Tailoring your presentation style accordingly, and keeping the others' in mind while listening, will facilitate your communication.

- Stating the obvious—articulating what you believe to be "understood" or acknowledging the elephant in the room—can be freeing for everyone involved.

- A lot of "show and tell/shock and awe" by others can be indicative of a weak argument or position. Before going to the mat with them, listen, empathize; this will often get you further than responding in kind.

- If you find you're facing a challenging situation, imagining how someone you admire might tackle it can help you find your footing.

- When you're feeling overwhelmed, breaking the "What next?" into words of one syllable can make the situation feel more manageable.

- Listen carefully to what others "joke" about—they're very rarely kidding.

- If someone's pushing your buttons, take an honest look at why. It might be something you find yourself doing that you're not that crazy about.

- Your voice mail message is often the first contact others have with you. Make sure it is welcoming and authoritative.

- Orchestrate your follow-up as carefully as you did your one-on-one encounter, even if it feels like the trail's gone cold. Persistence will often pay off.

## CHAPTER THREE

# Conspire to Inspire:
## Maximizing Meetings

I imagine many of you have looked at your calendar and thought, "Well, I'm not going to get much work done today. I'm in back-to-back meetings."

This is not good. It's possible this could make you feel a little nuts, because I don't know anyone who looks at a day that's got meetings stacked up like planes over LaGuardia (or O'Hare, or LAX, or Denver . . . take your pick) and rubs their hands together with glee.

This can change. Meetings can be fun again.

For me, an ideal meeting—a fun meeting—is one where everyone leaves the room with a clearer idea of both the team's objective and what their unique contribution to achieving that objective will be.

Because make no mistake about it, regardless of whether you are the leader of the meeting or a participant, you *do* have a unique contribution to make. And identifying that contribution will go a long way to changing your boss's, your colleagues', and—most important—your perception of yourself. You will find reserves of confidence, authority, and humor you never knew you had.

My goal with this section, then, is to help you maximize the time you spend in meetings. Implementing this information can make your meetings productive, efficient—even fun. You will find yourself thinking creatively, communicating clearly, negotiating smoothly. You will leave the room having presented your best self.

## Put It on a Matchbook

Have any of you had the experience of passing a coworker in the hall-way and having him ask you, "Where are you headed?" To which you respond, "Another marketing meeting . . . I'm not quite sure what it's about. . . ."

Few things in a workday are more draining than sitting through an interminable meeting, run by someone who hasn't had the time to prepare their presentation, or inquire into your needs and/or concerns.

At the other end of the spectrum is the meeting we lounge into only to discover we're suddenly on the hot seat, with questions being fired at us from all sides.

Here's my thinking: You should *never* attend any meeting for which you haven't prepared. Whether you're running the meeting or participating in it, you should have a clear idea of your objective/your team's objective/your company's objective. The question I like to ask myself is, "Is my objective so finely honed that I could put it on a matchbook cover?"

I often work in the film and television industry, and "Can you put it on a matchbook?" is a phrase you hear a lot, because if you can't explain the concept for your film or show in that small a space, it's unlikely it's going to get a strong response. Some taglines/plot descriptions from movies and television that offer great examples of this include: *Ghostbusters:* Plot—Three unemployed parapsychology professors set up shop as a ghost removal service. Tagline—"We're ready to believe you." *Grey's Anatomy:* Plot—A drama centered on the personal and professional lives of five interns and their supervisors. Tagline—"Operations. Relations. Complications."

You get the idea.

## Your Black Book for Meetings

In addition to being able to put your objective on a matchbook, you should also know the background and objectives of whoever else is in the room. Whether they're your colleagues or your competition, you need to know their goals, their concerns, and their style of listening so you can tailor your message and delivery and so, get the results you desire.

Why is this important? Because we're human beings, and that means we are influenced by far more than the EBITDA, the CAGR, or the PPE ratio. Given that, we respond to stories and examples that reference our lives and concerns: our kids, our dogs, our hobbies, our sports teams. . . . Taking the time to discover others' interests and referencing those interests in your presentations will inevitably bring you greater rewards.

Here's an example of how this information came in handy for one of my clients who'd gotten a call about appearing on *Oprah*. His conversation with the producers had left up in the air the question of whether or not the show would send a crew to come and shoot "B Roll" (secondary footage) in my client's office. Obviously, my client wanted this. The more material they had on him the better. In order to help them decide, they had asked my client to send some pictures of his office's interiors. My recommendation? Send a picture of you that includes the gigantic dog bed you keep in your office—and get the dogs back from the dog walker *right now*. Why? Because I (along with millions of other viewers) knew Oprah had just gotten three dogs. Bingo. The next call we got was that the producers were getting on a plane and coming to NYC.

So the next time you're preparing for a meeting with your competition, in addition to asking yourself: What's their best-selling product? What holes do they have in their research? Product line? Management? Also try to find out the human factors in play. Who's longing to be promoted? Who looks like they are on their way out the door? Who responds to examples with dogs? Cats? Children? Baseball? Sailing? Travel? Chess? Golf? Cooking?

It's this information that will humanize your presentation or idea—make it more colorful, more accessible, more meaningful to your listeners, and so, more likely to be remembered or accepted.

## Quarterback vs Closer

Almost any kind of sports reference is foreign to me. My knowledge of, and interest in, football centers almost exclusively on the kind of food you tend to get when people invite you over to watch a game—chips, potato salad, chili, nachos . . . all good.

That said, I do understand the function of the quarterback: to set up the play and instruct others where they need to be to complete it. This same idea is integral to an effective team presentation. One person needs to be designated to call the play in advance of the meeting, and to take the lead at its start. This person will also be the one team members should look to during the meeting should it become evident that a new play has to be called mid-game.

The benefit of beginning to think about team presentations in this way is that it ensures that, should there be a change in strategy, one member has been delegated to handle it—regardless. This doesn't mean he or she can't call a quick huddle to confer, but it does mean that the group will continue to present a unified front in the moment. Another benefit is that once other players understand their role—block, tackle, tight end (that's usually the finance guy . . .)—they get into a rhythm while presenting that comes across as seamless and controlled.

The other role it's important to delegate in advance is that of the closer—the person who's going to lean in at the end and ask for the money, the deal, the business. Why can't this request be made by the quarterback? In my experience, having the role change is beneficial for a number of reasons. The quarterback has given the overview of the field for everyone in the room. He or she has been compelling, inspiring, visionary—but now it's time to talk through the specifics of how it's going to get done. This abrupt change in tone can leave listeners feeling let down at best, or deceived at worst, when it's done by the quarterback. The big picture becomes suddenly mundane.

Another reason it can be beneficial to divvy it up is because some people respond to visionary, broad thinkers while others are very "grounded in reality" (as nursery school teachers describe the kids who want to make ornaments out of popsicle sticks rather than slay dragons in the dress up corner.) Having a variety of presentation styles ensures that everyone to whom you are presenting feels comfortable that they have a like-minded opposite sitting across from them.

The last reason I find it beneficial is because doing a presentation well—building a convincing, inspiring scenario—is exhausting. Asking one person to carry the ball all the way through is, to me, asking for trouble. This is often when a deal point gets dropped, an ill-considered remark is made, an opportunity is lost.

So, as you put together your strategy, also consider the role you will play. It goes a long way toward ensuring you end with a touchdown.

## Ally or Observer?

One of the questions I request my clients ask each other when they're presenting as a team is, "What do you need me to be in this meeting—an ally or an observer?"

What I mean by this is that once the team's leader has been declared or chosen, the rest of the team needs to take on one or the other—or sometimes both—of these roles.

When you're acting as an ally, your job is to sit next to those on your team and to look at whoever is speaking as if he is the most fascinating person you have ever met. Why? Because, as noted, 55 percent of your impact comes from the visual component of your presentation, and I'm not talking about your slides or your handouts. I'm talking about you. If you, as a team member, aren't visibly interested in what your team leader is saying, why should anyone listening to the presentation be interested? Many people in the room will take their primary cue from you.

If you've taken on the role of observer, your job is to take a constant inventory of the faces of those to whom you are presenting. Does she look bored? Does he look confused? Does she look disappointed? Does he look frustrated? Etc. Keeping an eye on these emotions allows you, then, during the question-and-answer portion of the meeting to ask questions such as, "I noticed that there seemed to be some confusion when Joe talked about X. Is there something we can clear up for you?" or "I noticed some of you seemed frustrated with our decision about Y. Is there some aspect of the problem we haven't addressed to your satisfaction?"

Working in this way has both immediate and long-term benefits. The people in the meeting will feel their questions and concerns were addressed in the moment, and they will leave feeling confident that you and your team are committed to staying on top of trouble-shooting going forward.

## Your Seat at the Table

So you've been invited to a new meeting. You walk into the room and there's a table with chairs around it. You sit yourself down in the nearest one and wham—you've sent a message to everyone in the room about what you perceive your role in the meeting will be.

Yes, it's true.

How can you tell which chair means what to whom?

The fact that the chair at the head of the table is the "power seat" is pretty obvious. If you're the one running the meeting, that's going to be the chair for you. But what about the other chairs? And what are you supposed to do if you're coming in as a team?

In my experience—as at a dinner table—the seat to the direct right of the person at the head of the table is the next most powerful place to be. After that, there is no clear hierarchical order, though it's true some people do jockey for the position at the foot of the table. (I once had a new client come into a meeting, see that I'd taken the chair at the head of the table—on purpose—and walk all the way to the chair at the foot of a gigantic conference room table to make his point about his perception of his equality in that meeting . . . .)

Other elements to consider are: where are the windows? If they're behind you, those across from you might be distracted by what's going on behind your head. Also, if it's a very sunny day, it makes it hard for people to look directly at you. Where's the door? If late-comers enter, you don't want them entering behind you and so, dis-tracting others from you, etc. (It's also nice to be able to send them a withering glance without having to turn your head.)

When I have clients presenting as a team my request is that they all sit side by side at one side of the table. Why? Because when team members don't sit next to one another, they send a mes-sage to everyone in the room that when they get back to the office, they aren't going to communicate easily with one another. The reason for this is that people who can't sit side by side don't "read" as comfort-able with one another. And who's going to believe that a team that isn't comfortable together is going to go back to the office and com-municate?

*Please note:* Although I rarely break things down along gender lines, this is one place I'm going to. Over the years I've been doing this work, I've noticed that in general—for reasons that are beyond the scope of this book—men are rarely comfortable sitting side by side. I'm here to tell you to get over it. Scattering yourselves around the table does you a huge disservice. If your team members object, feel free to tell them that I have made a few of my all-male teams give each other shoulder rubs to get themselves over it—because let's face it, after you've given your team members a shoulder rub, simply sit-ting side by side is pretty much a walk in the park.

## Hands Up!

While I've discussed the importance of being aware of your posture at the table, I am giving hand placement its own section in order to emphasize its importance in signaling your intentions to others.

As we all know, "Hands up!" is among the first things a police of-ficer says when he has a criminal in range. In that instance, the police officer's goal is to ensure he or she doesn't have a concealed weapon.

More happily, raising our hand is also the symbol of knowing the correct answer in grade school, or signaling our willingness to volunteer for activities as we get older.

When you are seated at a table, your hands perform much the same function. They allow others at the table to feel safe around you, and they signal to others that you are available and excited to answer their questions, or volunteer for their cause.

"But," some clients object, "I tend to talk with my hands if they're on the table. Isn't that bad?"

Not at all if those motions are a natural outgrowth of what you are saying. They only become distracting when they are doing something to relieve you of nervous tension, such as tapping a pencil or fiddling with a wedding ring, etc.

So if your goal is to inspire trust in others, one of the easiest ways to do that is to keep your hands where people can see them. Once they're on the table, my request is that they remain unclasped, as clasping your hands in front of you creates a barrier between you and those to whom you are speaking.

The same principle holds true if you are standing. When you want others to trust you, keep your hands out of your pockets. Leaving them in sight will signal your honorable, or favorable, intentions. Alternatively, putting your hands in your pockets will send a message of distrust or unavailability—not to mention ruin the line of your suit.

## The First-Date Gaze

Much of the work I do is with teams who are going out to pitch their company, their product, their idea. And the nature of pitching is that, as in baseball, you're going to be doing it more than once. In fact, it's likely you're going to be doing it over and over.

More often than not, I see that the consequence of listening to their colleagues say the same thing again and again means that other team members use this time—time when their team members are speaking—to check their PDAs, clean their nails, look out the window . . . .

This is not good.

Why? Because the fact that you aren't speaking does not mean you aren't presenting. As I've said before, if 55 percent of your impact is visual, and your *team members* can't even be bothered to listen to what you are saying, why should anyone across the table give you their cash?

Whether it's a new stock, a new telephone, or a new screenplay, my request of every team is that no matter how many times they have heard their team members tell the same story, they continue to look at whomever is speaking as if they are on a (good) first date. They need to be attentive, affirming, visibly engaged in the story they are hearing. They need to be listening as if it's the very first time they've heard the information.

"But what if it's the tenth or thirtieth or fiftieth time I've heard it?" I'm asked. "How can I possibly continue to look as if this is riveting to me?" Well, I tell them, if the possibility of a new client, or a new contract or a few million bucks isn't enough incentive, you can practice active, internal listening.

Active internal listening means that as your team member is speaking, you internally repeat everything they are saying *verbatim*. This forces you to listen with new ears, as if you have never heard this before.

Try it. The next time you are listening to your boss or your spouse or your friend tell a story that you've heard at least five, if not five hundred, times before, see if you can repeat it in your head as if your life depended on it—no missed ands, buts, or thes, much less missed critical information. This is particularly useful if it's a story you find incredibly dull.

What you'll discover when you begin listening to your team members this way is that the feedback you get from whomever you're presenting to is, "Wow, you guys really seem like a cohesive unit. I definitely got the sense you work as a team."

So whether you're attempting to sell your shares to possible investors, or sell yourselves as a cohesive parenting unit to a prospective school for your kids, practice the first-date gaze.

## Agree and Add

"Agree and Add" is a game that comes out of improv (that's theater improvisation to you and me). It also goes by the name of "Yes, and."

In improv, the purpose of Agree and Add is to keep the flow going. The idea is that no matter what has been said or done — no matter how disjointed or outrageous or counterintuitive it might have been — you are not allowed to do anything more than say, "Yes, and . . . ," and then it's up to you to take the action and the dialogue where you want them to go. You aren't allowed to do it by saying, "No," or "But," or "Hang on, I was thinking we were going to do it this way," etc.

Why is this a useful tool in meetings? Because there are few things that kill a team's credibility faster than having team members contradict one another during a presentation. If, for example, you are in the middle of making a point and one of the people on your team says, "No, Mike, what we discussed was X," it shuts everything down. In that moment, not only do you and your team member have to stop interacting with the client to sort out what you mean, but you also have to do it live, in real time, in front of the client. And even if you do manage that with a minimum of fuss, it can be hard to get your flow back — to remember where you were going when you were interrupted, and to feel confident in your ability to finish your portion of the presentation.

So what can you do if someone on your team has just said something that you know is incorrect, or isn't in line with what you had discussed ahead of time? There are a couple of options. If it's a small thing, let it slide. As they say in film and TV, "fix it in post" (that's "fix it in post-production" to you and me). In other words, depending on how egregious the error was, you can wait until your team member has finished speaking and use one of these phrases:

- "I wanted to add something to what Mike said . . ."
- "I wanted to clarify one point Mike made . . ."
- "I wanted to give you some additional background on a piece of the information Mike gave you . . ."

You get the idea.

If it's something that's too big to ignore—the figures are wildly incorrect, the schedule being discussed is impossible due to X, Y, and Z factors—my suggestion is that you interject this with the minimum of fuss. First, request a go-ahead from your colleague for making the interruption, "Mike, I need to interrupt for one second. Okay?" If you can smile while you do it, even better. Second, don't apologize or make excuses for the misinformation Mike just gave. Keep it simple. No one needs to hear how the figures changed after he went to bed, etc. Then, move quickly from the "what," i.e., "That schedule won't work," to the "because," "because of X, Y, or Z." If the problem can be sorted out there and then, do it. If not, you want to note it and move on. For example, "I wanted to flag that now. We'll discuss it after this meeting and confirm the new figures/schedule/whatever by the end of the day." Finally, you need to hand the ball back to your colleague. "That's all I wanted to clarify, now Mike can take you back to our production numbers for the next quarter," etc. In that moment, it's important to reestablish Mike's authority and credibility with the group.

So the next time you notice a team member, spouse, or boss veering off course, try to stifle the impulse to get them back on track with a verbal body check. Instead, Agree and Add.

## What's Working?

This is a lesson I picked up in a terrific magazine article I read a few years ago. As I'm not a research/footnote type, I didn't make a note of the magazine it was in, the name of the article, or the author of the piece. If you are that person, please let me know so you can get the credit you deserve.

What I do remember is that the thrust of the piece was how to solve problems more efficiently and effectively. The author recalled for readers the scene from *Apollo 13* where the scientists have gathered to figure out how they are going to get Tom Hanks, Kevin

### Keep It Behind Closed Doors

This is a phrase you hear a lot in the best dysfunctional families. You're at a party with your spouse and you're asked about a family member who's become the focus of unwanted notoriety, having ignited a local contretemps that's been cocktail party fodder for the last month. Or perhaps your partner triggers the argument that's been smoldering between you for the last fifteen years—insert your argument here. At this point, hopefully, someone has the sense to say, "Let's keep that behind closed doors."

While this may not do a lot for your mental health in the moment, it will do wonders for your family happiness in the long run.

The same sentiment applies in meetings where a team member inadvertently, or not, kick-starts an argument, discussion, or point of debate, that your team has been struggling with in the days or weeks prior to sitting down at the table. No matter how tempting it is to use that forum as a place to make your point, air your grievance, or simply shock and awe, don't do it. With teams, as with families, there are things that must be kept behind closed doors.

Bacon, and Bill Paxton back from space alive—and notes that the first question they asked about the equipment on the ship was, "What's working?"

Her point—now my point to you—is that when we have a situation that's tricky our first instinct is often to focus on what's not working as opposed to what is, and that this doesn't do a lot to facilitate problem-solving.

"But," you might be thinking, "if we don't talk about what's wrong how can we take steps to change it?" This is a valid question. In reply, however, please note that "What's working?" was just the first question they asked; it was not the only question they asked.

Unfortunately, however, beginning with the problem, the missteps, the drama seems to be the norm. It takes a cool head to step back and realize that not only does this waste time, but it also tends to lower morale. That from here it's generally just a few short steps to people feeling overwhelmed and consequently becoming belligerent, defensive, self-righteous, defeated, victimized—take your pick from a medley of distracting emotions.

So the next time you find yourself gathered around a conference room table preparing to triage the latest equipment breakdown/drop in the market/wardrobe malfunction, see if you can take a moment before you focus on what's not working to articulate what is. It might not make an enormous difference to the solution you discover, but it's more than likely it will help you arrive at that solution more quickly.

## "Can you tell me why you're doing it that way?"

A few years ago, I was teaching yoga quite a lot. And, as with many new teachers, I had a lot of ideas about how things "should" and "shouldn't" be done by my students—mostly, that things should be done exactly the way I said they should be done. Consequently, my internal dialogue when I saw someone doing something differently was, "What is wrong with you? Why aren't you listening to me?" (FYI: for all of you who are thinking yoga teachers shouldn't think this way: Yoga is a process. It's called yoga practice—not yoga perfect—for a reason. . . . It's also possible I'm a little tightly wound.) Over the years, however, as I took, and taught, more classes I realized that when I, or my students, were modifying something it was generally for a reason. I also realized that if a teacher corrected me without inquiring into my reason it made me cranky. This made life a lot easier for my students because it taught me the magic phrase, "Can you tell me why you're doing it that way?" which has been invaluable in multiple situations.

For example, recently I met with a client who was adamant about reading verbatim from a script that would appear on a teleprompter. So adamant that it was among the first things he told me, aggressively, when I got into the room. In that moment, it would have been easy to get my back up—to wonder why he had hired me if he was going to continue to work in the manner he always had. Instead, I pulled out the magic phrase: "Great. Can you tell me why you like doing it that way?" Although momentarily flummoxed by the lack of resistance, stories soon poured out of him. I realized he'd had some bad experiences and so, some justifiable anxieties. He realized I wasn't militant, or unsympathetic. At that point, we were in dialogue—not at loggerheads. And when you're in dialogue, the potential for change and compromise is far, far higher.

Another reason "Can you tell me why you're doing it that way?" is so useful is that it's just possible someone is doing it that way because they have misinformation or a better idea/more complete information than you do. In the former case, correcting them without inquiring can lead to bad feeling. It's possible they will be aggrieved

## You Really Shouldn't Have

These days, anytime I hear the word "should" in the context of "must" or "have to," I flag it as something that needs closer examination. The reason for this is that using "should" in these contexts is usually either the result of unexamined behavior (for example, "The napkins should be folded this way." Really? Was that written on one of the tablets Moses brought down from the mountain?) or it's the result of guilty feelings (for example, "I really should go visit my in-laws this weekend."). In both cases, "should" is being used inaccurately. In the case of the napkins, the correct phrasing would be, "I'd like you to fold the napkins this way." This is both accurate and it spares the feelings of the people whom you are directing—makes them feel less foolish for the choice they might have made. In the case of your in-laws, more appropriate phrasing might be, "I'm going to make a plan to visit my in-laws this weekend." Being factual allows you to remain honest with yourself and your spouse, which can make you both feel less aggrieved. You won't have tried to talk yourself into feelings that aren't genuine, and you won't have slipped into the danger zone of possibly offending him or her.

So if you find yourself or those around you using should, take a moment to delve deeper, and then, rephrase with greater precision.

at your assumption of their insubordination or incompetence. In the latter, you have an opportunity to learn something—always a plus.

## Avoid Handout Trap Hazards

In these days of proliferating computers and fluid typists, it's common to go to a meeting with a handout for others outlining the agenda, the upcoming season's sales strategy, the plan for industry-wide domination. Although I think we rely too much on our written work when presenting ideas—I am, after all, a speech coach—I'm resigned to the fact that it's often considered a must-have item.

What I'm not resigned to, however, is the flagrant reading-ahead by the majority of the people to whom the handout's given. People who flip ahead to see what's coming aren't, by definition, paying attention to what you're saying. If their internal monologue while reading is, "Okay, okay, okay, got it," they'll often check out mentally for the remainder of the meeting, missing important details for strategy implementation. If they bump into something they find surprising or upsetting, their mental attention generally remains on that. They stop listening to the plan for how to get there, focusing solely on their feelings about wherever "there" might be. The time spent on the "because" behind the idea becomes time wasted, and the big idea is greeted with anything from apathy to outright hostility.

I recommend instead putting together a one-sheet takeaway piece highlighting crucial statistics or strategies that can be given to attendees as they leave the meeting, and/or following up with an e-mail containing the same information. If you choose to do this, it can be helpful to announce that you're doing so at the outset of the meeting. This will save you from losing the attention of frantic note-takers or chronic doodlers.

If, however, you remain wedded to an in-meeting handout, either because of the familiarity of the process or the complexity of the material, I recommend prefacing handing it out by saying, "My request is we all stay on the page being discussed. Please don't flip ahead."

## "My request is"

Asking others to do something for us is uncomfortable for many of us. Consequently, we veer between the demanding-sounding, "I need you to do this," or the limp, "It would be great if you could do this." The former choice can get you the reputation of being ever so slightly dictatorial, while the latter can leave people commenting that you're a tiny bit passive aggressive—if you want something done, why not just say so? Given this, I gift you with the phrase, "My request is."

The beauty of "My request is" is that it leaves people in no doubt that a request has been made of them by you, but because you haven't used the "I/you" combination you avoid their feeling overwhelmed or beleaguered.

# "In the absence of orders, initiate appropriate action"

This is another Marine Corps phrase I adore and which, as a lack of accountability becomes more widespread—exemplified, to me, by the phrase, "My bad"—I long to have integrated into the general consciousness.

The value of this ethic both for corporate and personal good is undeniable. Here are top-down and bottom-up examples:

A few years ago I was lucky enough to hear Isadore Sharp, the CEO of The Four Seasons, speak. He told the audience that one of the biggest factors in their success is their policy of hiring based on attitude; that competence can be taught. He feels that this hiring mandate is among the reasons The Four Seasons has become the world's leading luxury hotel chain. Additionally, he told us that one of the biggest factors in both guest and employee satisfaction is their zero mistake policy: when mistakes inevitably occur, employees are trusted to use their common sense to turn mishaps into service opportunities.

The result? A win for guests as they get immediate rectification of a problem, without having to track down management. A win for employees, as they feel trusted by management to exercise their good judgment. And an overwhelming win for management, as they have both satisfied guests and satisfied employees.

Many years ago I had a client who was a trainee stockbroker at one of Manhattan's larger firms. One day he was in the men's room, which was littered with paper towels. He began picking them up. At that moment, one of the directors—a fairly Zeus-like figure—came in the bathroom and asked him what he was doing. He said he was picking up paper towels. The director asked why. He said because they were on the floor. The director pointed out that this wasn't his job. My client agreed but said that should a client come in, it would give them a poor impression of the firm.

Suffice to say that while this did not gain him immediate access to a corner office, his display of initiative did a lot to enhance his reputation with those occupying corner offices.

Too often we leave meetings without a clear sense of what our particular assignment is or could be—without having taken ownership of any piece of the action—simply because no one asked us directly to do so. As you can see, however, embodying and rewarding shows of initiative can be a pain- and cost-free way to move up in the ranks, inspire employee satisfaction, enhance revenues, and, last but certainly not least, allow you to fall asleep at night confident you did everything in your power to be your best.

## Putting the Constructive in Constructive Criticism

Ah, the performance review—that biannual or yearly meeting that so often seems to get postponed, interrupted, or cut short. I believe this is because although there are literally millions of ways to give people direction, feedback, criticism, it can be astonishingly difficult to both give and receive. Many of us dither or delay giving it for fear of further hampering the recipient's performance. Many of us are so shocked or distressed by the way in which we receive it, that we end up demoralized, further decreasing our motivation to excel. But if you can speak to the combination of those two elements— performance and motivation—when giving and receiving criticism, you'll find it far easier. Here's what I mean by this:

When I was teaching nursery school (yes, I have had a checkered career), among the most important points we stressed in the classroom, and to the parents, was never to say, "Good boy" or "Good girl." Instead, we would say, "I really liked the way you shared the truck with your friend," or "Thank you for washing your hands before snack." Similarly, we never said, "Bad boy," or "Bad girl." Instead, "I need you to start picking up the blocks when I tell you it's clean up time," or "You may not grab the book from your friend."

The reason for this is that tying behavior to character is dicey. Although they can't articulate it, approaching discipline in this way causes children to begin to question themselves: are they only a good person when they do things correctly or exactly as they're told? Are they a bad person if they make a mistake or disobey you? In either case, it's unlikely they're going to feel like a "good person" for long. And once they think they have nothing to lose—that you've made up your mind about their character—their motivation to listen to you and change their behavior lessens day to day.

As hard as it may be to admit sometimes, deep down we haven't changed that much from the people we were in nursery school. We like stories, we like snacks, we like routine intermixed with brightly colored new toys and field trips. And we perform best when criticism is depersonalized the way it was then. When we receive it in the form of, "You always do X, and I've told you a million times to do Y," or "When I ask you to do Z, that doesn't mean in an hour/a day/a week. You need to do it now," we lose motivation. If, however, the behavior is detached from the implication about our personality—that we're forgetful, we're lazy, etc—the chances of that behavior changing both in the moment and in the future improve considerably. Given this, tie criticism to process, not personality. "Y is quicker/easier/

cheaper than X. Please do it that way. X is not a choice." "Z needs to happen now. It's now, now."

Another critical piece in effective, constructive criticism is to lay out your expectations in writing with your colleague, and have a conversation with him about his understanding of exactly what is meant by them, both at the time of hiring and at regularly scheduled intervals during his tenure. The critical piece here is to have both written and discussed them. If you simply hand someone a sheet of paper or shoot him an e-mail, it's too easy to have your direction misinterpreted. If you rely solely on conversation, the same is true, and you have no record of what was agreed on. In my ideal world, both people work together on, and sign, a performance expectation document. This keeps misunderstandings to a minimum, and enhances partnership.

# S.M.E.A.C.

Ah, S.M.E.A.C.—a part of our family lexicon once again borrowed from the Marine Corps.

What is S.M.E.A.C.? It's an easy, intuitive mental framework for efficiently conveying information to a group of people about an upcoming task. Once you've used it a few times, it comes naturally, and gives you a great mental checklist to ensure that no planning essentials get missed. S.M.E.A.C. stands for:

*Situation*—We've got to prepare a sales proposal for a new prospect at short notice.

*Mission*—To ensure that the plan that we prepare wins us the sale. (In the Corps, this also includes "Commander's Intent": this is especially important, because if everyone knows the overall mission—as opposed to just "do this by then"—then there is scope for individual judgment and initiative if the situation changes.)

*Execution*—Tom will gather data about the prospect's formal requirements; Frances will gather information about who will be judging the proposal; John will be responsible for doing the graphical aspects of the presentation; we will then gather and do a first draft three days before the presentation is due.

*Administration and Logistics* (a.k.a. Bullets, Beans, and Band Aids)—What we'll need to get the job done—We're assembling in Tom's offices next Tuesday at 9 A.M.; Frances is responsible for providing the laptop, dry erase board and pens for brainstorming; John is bringing the coffee. Keep receipts for any expenses incurred, as the client says that they will reimburse these if we file them following the presentation.

*Communication*—This is how we are going to stay in touch while executing the mission. E.g., any problems before Tuesday, use e-mail; if anyone gets held up on the day, give the rest of the team a call.

Why is S.M.E.A.C. helpful? Because it can provide you with an easy structure for talking with your team about accomplishing a set objective. For example, say your boss comes to you and says you and your team need to get a report written and presented to him within forty-eight hours. Having the S.M.E.A.C. framework is a great way to keep everyone from focusing on the deadline, and instead, focus them on the steps needed to meet the deadline. Not only do you manage morale better this way—preventing everyone from dropping into Chicken Little, "the sky is falling!" mode—you ensure everyone is clear on what they need to accomplish and that no piece is dropped getting it done.

Given my line of work, I found the next bit incredibly interesting, though not really surprising. My brother told me that in the Corps the most often overlooked piece is communication—how do you plan to stay in touch during the process? What checkpoints are you going to have in place to ensure everyone is meeting their deadline on time and/or can alert you immediately if they aren't? How often will those checkpoints occur? This kind of ongoing communication is critical to ensuring that you don't all arrive, breathless, in the room at the final hour only to have one person say, "Okay, I didn't tell you this earlier, because I couldn't find you, but I wasn't able to find X, or do Y."

That's never a good moment.

While it can seem overly contrived from time to time, I can't tell you how many times it's saved me from dropping the ball when there was no room for error. It also makes you look incredibly together and organized if you're put in charge of a temporary team that has been given an impromptu task that needs doing in a hurry: you just jump right in with "The situation is X; our mission is Y; we'll make that happen through A, B, and C . . ."

Believe me: When you finish a SMEAC and ask "Any questions?" people will be impressed!

## SUMMING IT UP:

- Clarify and focus your meeting's objective tightly enough that you could write it on a matchbook cover.

- Consider more than the bottom line when you're researching a project. Know who will be in the room and the "human factors" in play.

- Designate who will be quarterbacking the meeting and who will be closing it before you walk in the room.

- Choose or assign the roles of ally or observer to other team members, then follow through on the attributes of each.

- Where you choose to sit at a table sends as strong a message to everyone in the room as what you might say. Choose wisely.

- If you want others' trust, keep your hands where they can see them.

- If you aren't speaking you need to be looking at whoever is as if you're on a (great) first date.

- Use "Yes, and" to transition, as opposed to "No" or "But."

- When a situation or problem feels impossible, begin by focusing on what's working.

- Don't assume you know why others are modifying or changing your instructions. Ask why before jumping to conclusions.

- Distribute handouts at the end of a meeting, not before. If this is impossible, request up front that everyone stay on the same page.

- When you see something that needs doing, take the initiative and tackle it yourself. Don't wait to be told.

- Tie constructive criticism to process, not personality. Rather than, "You can't procrastinate. Do X immediately," "X needs to happen now."

- Make sure all team members are clear on the S.M.E.A.C: Situation, Mission, Execution strategy, Administration needs, and Communication pipeline for every project.

## CHAPTER FOUR

# Interview to a Kill:
## Stress-Free Job Interviewing

Job interviews. Root canal. For a lot of people, it would be hard to choose which they'd rather avoid more.

Myself, I've been on a *lot* of interviews and I used to dread them. Being asked a question for which I hadn't prepared would leave me mentally kicking myself. Encountering resistance I hadn't imagined encountering would leave me wanting to kick them. For example, when I was first interviewing in publishing one editor told me she wouldn't feel comfortable hiring me because I was too old to be asked to go out to the pharmacy and buy her cigarettes. I was left with my mouth opening and closing like a goldfish—with nothing coming out.

I know one of the reasons I didn't use to prep extensively ahead of time was because the stakes were so high. I'd want the job so much that thinking about it would make me nervous and so I'd procrastinate, or tell myself I did better off the cuff . . . .

The trouble with this is, hope is not a strategy.

For inspiration in moments like these, it helps me to think of Rabindranath Tagore's quote: "Let me not pray to be sheltered from dangers, but to be fearless in facing them." This fearlessness comes as you begin to realize that you do have far more control over the interview process than you realized. Knowing the company's background can help you anticipate your interviewer's questions and help you formulate terrific questions of your own. Doing your "I've sat where you're sitting" homework can help you anticipate any reservations they might have and prepare how you will ameliorate them.

This is the purpose of this chapter: to help you feel confident that you can handle anything that comes at you—to leave you actually looking forward to the tough questions. To fire you with a "Bring it on!" attitude that will inspire both you and your future employer.

## What Three Words . . .

Prior to every coaching session, I ask clients to complete a short questionnaire. Among those questions:

- What three words would you use to describe yourself?
- Has anyone ever commented on these qualities, positively or negatively?
- What three words would you like your interviewer to use to describe you when you are finished meeting?

The purpose of this is to help me understand how my clients perceive themselves, to clear up any misconceptions they, or others, may have about these qualities, and to give them a focus for what will help them achieve their goals in the moment.

For example, a word I gave myself when I did this exercise was talkative. When I checked that perception against my friends' perception of me, I was shocked. Over and over I was told that their first impression of me was reserved, shy, quiet. It was only after getting to know me that they discovered how much I had to say.

When I applied this information to an interview situation, I had an "aha" moment. As most companies are looking for confident, outgoing, interactive-types—and I initially come across as reserved—it was no wonder I wasn't getting the second interview. Interviews typically occur in a very finite amount of time. Consequently, my interviewers never saw me as a viable candidate; there wasn't time for them to get to know how responsive I can be.

Armed with this information, I made the decision to step outside my personal-interaction comfort zone in my next interview. I "opened" with outgoing, interactive, and engaging.

Was this easy? No. It took practice. But this practice paid off in spades for me—and it can for you, too. So, choose three words you want your interviewer to use about you when you leave the room. Do you want them to say you are confident? Informed? Reliable? Tenacious? Flexible? A leader?

Once you have these in hand, ask yourself, and some reliable friends, are these words that spring to mind to describe me? If not, don't panic. I promise you that you have them. They might not be the qualities you "open" with, but they are available to you. "I am what I am" worked for Popeye because he was a cartoon character, but human beings have infinite potential. This includes you. You have the ability to express whatever qualities are needed to present your best self in any situation. If the words your friends offer you don't describe qualities you feel would serve you in an interview situation, challenge yourself to step outside your comfort zone, to practice embodying attributes that will demonstrate this infinite potential to others.

## Check for Tone Deafness

So many times we head into a situation thinking we know the attitude or behavior it calls for. Alternatively, we have an idea about the kind of person who gets the job. For example, traders on the floor of the New York Stock Exchange are aggressive and outspoken, nursery school teachers are nurturing and compliant, etc. The trouble with this way of thinking comes when we get so wedded to our idea of what behavior or attitude is appropriate, that we end up missing or ignoring the qualities that would serve us better in that moment. We become attitudinally tone deaf.

One of the more dramatic examples of this misunderstanding of the range of qualities needed to succeed occurred with a client who came to me to prepare for job interviews, having lost millions in investors' money on a self-started Internet venture. When I asked him how he would describe himself, he talked about being aggressive, alpha, outspoken. He was confident that these qualities would stand him in good stead during the interview process—would show potential employers that he was still tough, still had nerve. His response to the question, "Why should a prospective boss hire you?" was, "I'm not afraid of risk. I may have failed but at least I tried."

The trouble was that as he spoke his body language was all over the place. He was shifting side to side, leaning in too close, lolling back in his chair, looking out the window . . . .What this said to me was that although he had an idea about this tactic being effective, this answer wasn't comfortable for him. If he went into an interview with this answer, his interviewer wouldn't trust him; he might not be able to articulate why he didn't trust him, but he wouldn't trust him.

Over the course of the day we talked a lot about what it was like to show up for people as aggressive, alpha, outspoken, etc. Were there times, people, situations, in which being "softer" would have been a more effective choice? At that point he told me the story of having put on a very sharp suit to go tell one of his investors—an elderly woman—he had lost her money. He told me he'd been sorry afterward, that this choice about how someone in his situation should act had put an enormous barrier between them. He said he wished he'd made a choice that looked more accessible, and so conveyed more compassion, more accountability.

At the end of the day when I questioned him again about why a prospective boss should hire him his response was, "Because I know the value of a dollar. I know what it means to lose investors' retirement money, or the money for their children's education, and I will never let that happen again." As he spoke, his body didn't shift. He looked me in the eye. I assume he did as well in the interview, because he got the job.

So how can you check yourself for tone deafness? One way is to look at the words you'd use to describe the attitude you think would be most effective for the situation or position. If you notice that they are all in the same emotional family, it's likely you could stand to re-think your approach because there are very few jobs that require a one-note response. In fact, in the same way the majority of life re-quires fluidity of self-expression, your job will, too. Demonstrating for an interviewer that you have access to a variety of ways to handle coworkers, deadlines, and pressures, is infinitely more reassuring to them—even a circus doesn't want a one-trick pony.

## Know Your Softball Swing

I often work with magazine editors. One of the seemingly easy ques-tions we prepare for is what's known as a "softball question," i.e., "Tell me about your magazine." (Yes, I know this isn't technically, gram-matically, a question—it's an "upspeak" statement that demands an answer—but you get the idea.) These are known as softballs because the possibilities for how to answer are so numerous people don't know what to swing at. This happens a lot at cocktail parties, too. The next time you hear someone ask, "Read any great books lately?" look around and watch people's minds go blank. . . .

A softball question is a seeming conversation-starter that, in fact, is a conversation-stopper. They happen a lot on television because hosts are often so inundated with meetings and materials that their prep-time is reduced to minutes, if not moments.

How should you handle these? Go immediately to a specific. In the case of the magazine editors, they replied, "In this issue, I'm most excited about our article on Y."

So what will your softball swing look like? If you're a business owner, the question might be something along the lines of, "Tell me about your business." Your swing, "My favorite thing about the busi-ness is X." If you're a writer, and the question is "Tell me about your book." Your answer, "I wrote X because I'd always been interested in Y." (Or because there was such confusion around the subject, or be-cause there wasn't a resource of this kind available . . . you get it: It's the story of your impetus for writing the book.) If you're at a job interview and the question is "Tell me about your last job," your go-to is "My favorite thing about my last job was . . ."

Anticipating, and preparing for, the inevitable softball question will give you the "go-to" answer that will allow you to be calm, confident and—most important—memorable.

## What's the Worst That Could Happen?

In the same way I encourage clients to be able to articulate three words they want others to use about them once the interview or meeting is over, I also ask clients to spend time preparing strategies for the worst three situations, or the answers to the worst three questions they can imagine being asked during an interview or Q & A. I call this "Opposition Prep" because if you're concerned about something, it's not enough to hope it doesn't come up. It's far better to be on offense than defense.

Here's an example of what this might look like: I had a client who'd been out of the public eye for years, but was now making her comeback. Part of the public's institutional memory about her was a quote she gave in one of her last interviews that "read" as indescribably obnoxious. (Suffice to say, if I gave you the quote, you'd remember the person.) She'd just discovered that the journalist who had done that interview was writing her comeback story, and she was freaked, not only because her initial contact had gone poorly but also because there were now some open secrets she simply would not discuss.

I asked her what her strategy was going to be. She said she'd had her team call him and tell him if he wrote anything bad about her, they'd cut off his hands. . . . I said, "Okay, that's definitely one option . . . but maybe you want to think about getting on offense instead of defense." I suggested that rather than going in and saying "I can't believe it's you," it might be more helpful to go in and say, "I was so *glad* when I heard it was you. . . . I've changed so much in the last few years—as I'm sure you have—and since you knew me then, who better to talk about how much I've changed?" *And* to lean in and smile while she said it—you can never underestimate the 55 percent. His response? He sat back, loosened his collar, and said, "Wow . . . I came in here expecting a fight. Do you mind if I have a cigarette?" From then on, she had him in the palm of her hand and gave the interview of her life—one which, when it was published, permanently changed the public's perception of her.

## Your Black Book for Interviews

Boy oh boy do I wish someone had given me this information before I began the interview process. I can't tell you how much more impressive I would have been when I went to interview—I can't tell you how many more jobs I would have gotten!

Here's what I see as the biggest misconception about interviews: We think that going on interviews is primarily going to entail us talking about ourselves.

It's not.

Going on interviews is about us talking about how we fit into the corporate mission and culture of the company we're interviewing to work with.

What I mean by this is that we are rarely being hired for our value as a stand-alone product. We are being hired for what we can add to the company as it currently exists. We are, essentially, a "gift with purchase" for our future boss, the business's customers, the company's shareholders. We are being hired to improve their lives and their bottom line.

As you can see, this approach drastically changes the way you might approach the interview process. Hopefully, it motivates you to compile your black book.

What goes into that? A whole lotta research.

Here are some of the questions it's important to ask in this situation:

- What is the company's mission statement?
- What have the company's earnings looked like over the past five years?
- What's their best-selling/signature product? Why?
- What's their newest product/acquisition/success? Why was it so successful?
- Who is their biggest competitor? What is *their* best-selling/signature product? How does it compare?
- Do you see any gaps in their current strategy? If you do, what solutions can you offer for responding to those gaps?
- Who makes up the top management team? What's their business background? What's their educational background? What's their personal background? Is there any overlap with your background? Do you share neighborhoods, former schools, similarly-aged children?
- What does the corporate culture look like? Formal? Low key? Down and dirty? How does that mesh with your personality?
- Do you fulfill all the stated requirements for employability? If you do, what qualities—unique to you—will enhance the job you will do for them? If you don't, what qualities unique to you are going to make up for that shortfall?

As you can see, there's a lot that goes into the prep. Thankfully, there's a lot that can come out of it. The fact that you've taken the time to do this kind of background check is impressive to an interviewer. The fact that you might share similar tastes, interests, schools, hobbies might be the deciding factor in choosing between you and another candidate with similar credentials. Finally, actively demonstrating how you, and you alone, can offer the best "gift with purchase" can seal the deal—leave your interviewer saying, "Not only do you have everything we're looking for, your experience/background/skill set is a value-added we hadn't even considered. You've got the job."

## If You're on Time, You're Late

While it may seem absurd to have to stress the importance of arriving on time for your job interview, experience has taught me that this isn't so. I know people who have shown up anywhere from five minutes late to not at all. While I'm not prepared to tackle the hows and whys of those who haven't shown up—that's a level of self-sabotage I think should be handled by someone with a medical degree—I am willing to state for the record that in an interview situation, if you're on time, you're late.

What, then, do I recommend? In an ideal world I prefer that you be in the vicinity of the interview at minimum fifteen minutes ahead of schedule. This will give you the chance to find parking, see if you're going to need to clear security in the lobby, navigate a plethora of elevator banks, get yourself to an upper floor, etc. If none of these conditions is a factor, simply find a quiet spot to sit and collect yourself. Tell the assistant you're there but there's no need to announce you as you're a few minutes early. (Don't underestimate the importance of finding out the assistant's name and batting around a few pleasantries. If you don't think your prospective boss won't ask him or her which candidates were considerate in this way, you're mistaken.) Have yourself announced five minutes before your interview.

## Beware Being "Too cool for school"

Cool's been around forever, and—like pornography—it doesn't have a distinct definition, though most of us know it when we see it. The trouble with combining cool and a business environment occurs when we translate the cool that garnered us the attention of the popular girl or guy in high school into a working situation. Let me give you an example:

One day I got a call from a client asking me if I would come in and look at one of their employees who—although consistently interviewed for TV opinion pieces—never made the cut to the final show.

They couldn't figure it out: he was knowledgeable, handsome, articulate . . .

As you can imagine, this is my idea of catnip. In I went. In came
the client. He was indeed handsome. He shook hands with me, sat
down, crossed one leg so his ankle was on his opposite knee, threw
one arm over the back of the chair, tilted himself waaay back,
opened his mouth. . . . My work was done. He was "too cool for
school."

It's always important to be aware of your physicality—how you
are taking up space. Leaning way back in your chair, throwing your
arm over the back of a chair, putting one ankle on top of your other
knee so you give your listener a crotch shot, all "reads" for your
viewer as "I am way too cool to be here." Everything that comes out
of your mouth after that is almost superfluous.

Although we worked on some messaging that day, my primary advice to him was to sit forward in his chair, keep both his feet on the
floor, lean in, and smile. The result? The very next piece he taped
got used. He was thrilled. His bosses were thrilled. And I'm sure (if
you're a moviegoer) you are thrilled because he gives great advice
about going to the movies. He just didn't know the best way to get
that advice across.

The above is true regardless of whether it's television or not. If
you are on a job interview, regardless of your verbal smarts or your
credentials, this type of physicality is probably going to put
your interviewer off. They'll go back to HR and say, "Yes, his résumé
was great—impeccable really—and he had answers for every question . . . but do you have anyone else I can meet? He just didn't seem
like a team player."

So although I have no quarrel with you acting out your definition
of cool on your own time—on your town's Main Street or in its
hottest nightclub, on a date or at a class reunion, in front of your
bathroom mirror or in the shower—please don't break it out when
the consequence might be more than a failing grade.

# If You Can't Fix It, Feature It

The first time I heard this phrase was at a cocktail party. Someone said, "Group picture—look this way!" The gentleman next to me said, "I *do not* like having my picture taken. Look at the size of my nose! But—if you can't fix it, feature it." Then he turned to the camera and gave the photographer an enormous smile.

"Wow," I thought. "Cut. Print."

The trouble with a perceived problem is that we often spend a lot of time thinking of ways to distract others from noticing it. You see this a lot with fashion—we'll wear flat front pants to look thinner or vertical stripes to look longer. Instead of working to embrace a perceived flaw, self-consciousness, shame, or devotion to an unrealistic fashion ideal will make us prisoners in our own bodies. Making the choice to feature it can make all the difference, however.

For example, when Jennifer Lopez was just breaking out, she trumpeted to the world that her "signature" assets were her curves. Rather than trying to distract us from them, or cover them up, she went front and center with them. Her decision—to take a situation where the difference between her own body and the current trends in fashion could have been a constant source of conversation and frustration and instead say to the world, "Get on board, or get out of my way"—worked. The world got on board.

If you're thinking that that's all very well for celebrities, I'll give you an example from one of my clients. We met because he was interviewing for a new job in banking. The reason he called me was that he'd been out of work for a while, and—before that—had moved from firm to firm to firm. In his interviews, this kept being raised as a problem. It "read" for interviewers as incompetence on his part. In reality, he'd just had the misfortune to land more than once at a firm that went through a merger while he was there. And the fact is that when two banks get together, a lot of people go. What I told him was that since his history couldn't be changed, he needed to change how his history was perceived.

How did we do this? We decided to feature it. In his next interview I told him to bring it up as soon as possible. Say, in fact, that he wasn't interested in the job if a future merger was in the offing because he simply didn't want to go through that again. And the truth is it really *was* important to him to find a stable situation. The trouble was that he wasn't featuring it. When he did, he got what he asked for.

So the next time you find yourself or your team running into a situation that common sense or your corporation or society might tell you to ignore, downplay, or cover up, flip your thinking. Ask yourself, "What would I do if I wanted to give this a starring role?" What you thought was a problem, might just be a solution.

### The Power of the Pause

One constant to every answer is the importance of pausing before you begin to speak.

Why is this particularly important in an interview situation?

When you're interviewing for a new job, the stakes are high. You want to seem very prepared, informed, enthusiastic. A side effect of this is that you jump on every question—hurrah, I know that! The downside to this is that you can find yourself halfway through your answer with no idea where you're headed, and—while you may come across as eager—it's more likely you'll come across as immature or anxious.

Pausing before you begin to speak gives you time to collect your thoughts and "reads" for your interviewer as more authoritative.

So, here's how it goes:

*Interviewer:* Looking down at your résumé, "Tell me why you left your last job?"
*You:* Wait for your interviewer to look up at you. Inhale. Lean in. Open mouth. Begin well-crafted response . . .

Why wait for him or her to look up? Because when the question's tough, you want them to know you didn't blink.

# The Underrated Informational Interview

When I was thinking about switching professions, from teaching to publishing, I kept going on interviews and striking out. I couldn't figure it out. There had to be something I was doing incorrectly, but what was it? To discover, I began going on informational interviews—setting up meetings with people whom I would have loved to have as bosses, but who weren't looking for help. I figured they might be able to tell me how to crack the code. This turned out to be invaluable; this turned out to be how I made the jump.

The purpose of an informational interview is to find out both what a boss in your field is looking for and—just as important—what they are not. Also, to discover what their concerns might be from looking at your résumé.

Here's an example: when I began the process of breaking into publishing, I was the ripe old age of twenty-five. I'd been teaching for four years and had gotten a master's degree. From where I sat, that made me a great candidate. From where a future boss sat, that made me a liability. I discovered their concern was that no sooner would they get me trained to their liking than I would move on. Also, that I wouldn't be comfortable doing the kinds of jobs that assistants in publishing are routinely required to do: Xerox manuscripts, file, "go out to the Duane Reade and buy my cigarettes," as one woman told me. (She was right about that one, actually.) Knowing this, I was able to go into an actual interview and say, "I understand that my age and experience might be a concern—that you feel I might leave in a few months. I can tell you that I'm willing to make an eighteen-month commitment to this job once you offer it to me."

Bingo.

Another question to ask in your informational interview is what *not* to say—in fact, that can be as important as asking what you should say. Over the years I have found that in every industry there is one question you can ask, or statement you can make, that just drives people *wild*.

For example, when I worked in publishing that phrase was, "And

I know my book would be great on *Oprah*." Aaaaauugh. I mean, their book might very well be great on *Oprah*—but getting your book on *Oprah* is a bit like getting struck by lightning. The effect of a prospective author saying this was only to make everyone in the room think, "High maintenance. Possibly delusional. Back away slowly."

When I began to produce theater, I went on a few informational interviews with established producers and asked them the same question. It seems that in theater, the hot button statement is, "And this could also make a *great* screenplay." This is their "Aaaaaaugh" statement because if it would make a great screenplay, then why are you pitching it as theater? They are two very different animals. It drives the meeting right into the ground.

The fact that the interview is informational doesn't mean you don't have to prep just as carefully as you would if there were a job at stake. You should know your interviewer's résumé inside and out, plus have as much "soft" information on them as possible: hobbies, children's ages, etc. You should have a list of questions you'd like to have answered: are there any skills I should fine-tune? Are there any immediate red flags you see when you look at my résumé? Are there any new trends in the industry I should be aware of? Are there any idiosyncrasies in the industry I should be aware of? As noted above, is there anything I should absolutely never, ever say?

Now it might seem that people in these positions don't have the time or energy to give to these interviews. I rarely found this to be true. As long as you make it clear that you will require no more than fifteen minutes of their time, and it can be done on-site, it's unlikely you'll be turned away. The people I know who've been shut down had often opened with, "Let me take you to lunch." While this is a lovely offer, these people are busy. They don't want to commit to lunch. So, set yourself up for success by respecting their time limits up front.

Two other great benefits of this kind of interviewing are that once you get an interview with someone in their field, you can often call back and ask if there's anything in particular about that person it would be important for you to know. Also, if they were sufficiently impressed with you, they will have you in mind when someone in their industry is looking to hire a new person for their team.

Informational interviews are a win/win/win—and all those wins are for you. You get the experience of interviewing, you get the information, and you get the future connection.

## Now It's Your Turn

We're often so intent on proving a job is right for us that we forget to consider why we are right for the job, until our interviewer asks the seemingly innocuous question, "So, why do you think we're the right firm for you?"

FYI: This is not a good time to go blank.

Doing due diligence on why you're right for the job is just as important as researching why the job is right for you. In order to get the job that fits your needs, you need to walk into the room with a clear set of priorities regarding what you value in terms of teamwork, autonomy, and benefits.

For example, when I was younger I really enjoyed having a boss that acted as a mentor—someone very hands-on, very good at constructively criticizing and guiding the work I did. Knowing this was a dynamic that worked for me made it easier to articulate my desire for this type of setup; to let potential employers know I felt they were invaluable for learning not only the ins and outs of the industry, but my own strengths and weaknesses as well. In return I was willing to offer my particular brand of competitiveness, which was that I would never walk into their office and simply tell them about a problem. Rather, I was someone who would walk in, tell them about a problem, and offer at least two solutions for them to consider.

As they say, that was then, this is now. These days I'm not such a fan of being told how it's going to be done, which is why I'm now my own boss. The price I pay for this, of course, is being my own boss; which, in addition to a tad more insomnia, means that I'm now also responsible for my payroll, my health insurance, my retirement plan . . . who's luckier than me?

But back to you. Aside from the standard questions about salary and health insurance, what are some of the questions I recommend you think about asking yourself and your future employer?

- How much communication do I require/can I tolerate during the day?
- How much communication does my future boss require during the day?
- What form of communication (e-mail/instant message/ telephone/face-to-face) do I prefer?
- What form does my future boss prefer?
- How much direction do I need/can I tolerate in the midst of an intense project?
- How closely does my future boss like to monitor his employees during projects?
- Is it "understood" that 9–5 really means 8–7?
- Is that going to work with my schedule?
- Is there the possibility of future flex time?
- How much do I value that possibility?
- How often will my job performance be reviewed?
- What are the criteria by which I will be reviewed?
- What are the possibilities regarding bonuses and/or raise increments at that time?

Considering these kinds of questions up front will help you both in the moment—show your interviewer the thought you've given to the position—and down the road. Because walking in with a clear idea of your priorities means you won't be looking for a new job six months after you shake on this one.

## Know Your Walk-Away Number

Very often when we go in for a job interview, we're so focused on get-ting the job that we don't stop to consider whether the salary is, in fact, commensurate with our skill set. We don't enter the interview with a "walk-away number"—the number below which we won't take the job.

This is important. This isn't just a luxury for people who don't need the job in order to survive. I think that regardless of the finan-cial situation you're in when you enter the interview, it's important to have picked out a walk-away number.

The first reason for this is the mental edge it gives you. It's impor-tant to recognize your skill set is valuable regardless of whether or not it's acknowledged as being so by others, and regardless of the state of your bank balance. One of the best statements I've ever heard made about this came from Russell Crowe (if you're surprised by the way that sentence ended, you are surely not more surprised than I was when I heard him say it.) During his *Inside the Actor's Studio* inter-view he was talking about being in dire financial straits after finishing *L.A. Confidential*. Although he was getting multiple offers for parts in television shows and movies, he didn't take them because they weren't up to the standards he held for himself. His exact statement was, "You have to back your own talent." I love that. I think it's true. I think it's hard to ask someone else to back your talent if you aren't willing to do so yourself. Walking in secure in that belief will show up for your interviewer as confidence, poise, grace under pres-sure . . . multiple important qualities.

The second reason for having a walk-away number is that if the salary they're offering you isn't up to the number you've chosen, and you haven't picked out a walk-away number, you can be so relieved when you're offered anything at all that you say yes without further negotiations. And further negotiations are valuable for a number of reasons:

They're valuable because the number you've been offered is often just the company's opening bid and they expect you to ask for more. If you don't, you lose. They aren't going to point out to you, "No, now you're supposed to counter offer."

They're valuable because if the offer is final, they might be willing to build in a review in six months, during which they would add X amount based on your performance. If you haven't given some thought to what X amount might be, you could easily lowball yourself in the pressure of the moment.

And finally, it's important to have a walk-away number for just that reason—so you know when to walk away and continue looking for something that pays you what you're truly worth.

## You Don't Ask, You Don't Get

For many of us, the idea of asking outright for what we want or deserve is extremely foreign. We've been raised in one of two schools: "Virtue is its own reward" or "Life's not fair." Given that, we look through our closet for our martyr or victim hair shirt and put that on. We say things like, "I don't want to seem cocky." Or, "I don't see the point; it'll never happen."

I'm here to tell you it doesn't have to be this way, and it can't be.

Asking for what you want in terms of salary, benefits, flex time is a must. Not doing so means you'll be disgruntled, and no one wants an employee with a chip on his shoulder any more than you want to have one. (Unless, of course, that's your thing—but that's an area in which I'm not qualified to advise you, as dearly as I might like to.)

So the issue then becomes how to ask. Often, we've spent so much time fine-tuning our martyr/victim skill set that we've neglected learning how to make a request in a way that conveys respect for ourselves as well as respect for the person with whom we're negotiating.

What to do? Here is the best pointer I can give you:

Recognize that more often than not "no" is just information. It is not a reflection on your character, your appearance, your value to the firm. In other words, as much as you may want to believe it, it's very rarely personal. In fact it's far more likely to be a reflection on the history of the position or the current balance sheet of the company. Understanding this will make it infinitely easier not only to make your request, but to make it in a way that doesn't "read" as belligerent, subservient, passive-aggressive, etc.

For example, if you were to ask about working from home on Fridays and were told, "No," without an explanation, you might be inclined to think your employer doesn't trust you to get your work done, which might, in turn, make you upset as you have yet to prove yourself untrustworthy. Further inquiry might reveal, however, that this is a company-wide policy based on past experience with their employees—it has no bearing whatsoever on what they think about your qualifications. Keeping this idea in mind as you probe for more information will mean your tone and body language will remain under your control throughout the conversation: you won't seize up or lash out.

In these moments, your personal comfort with the material will put your interviewer at ease, which will keep you at ease. And a mind that's at ease is relaxed and fluid enough to roll with the punches—to convey confidence and humor, two essential elements in the negotiation process.

## The Polished Follow-Up

Most of us spend a lot of time thinking about what we need to do to get ready for an interview, but few of us spend much time thinking about how we're going to follow up afterward. How we follow up is critical, however, particularly if an employer is wavering between two applicants. In those instances a well-worded, timely note can tip the balance in your favor.

What should this note look and sound like? Its particulars will always be decided by the industry and people in question, but there are some things I insist on, and a few things I like to see:

- It must arrive within twenty-four hours.
- While I am a fan of snail mail, e-mail has become so pervasive that it no longer carries any stigma, so while I believe snail mail is a way to stand out from the crowd, e-mail is fine.
- My request is that it not begin with, "Thank you so much for meeting me yesterday." As an opening it lacks both originality and confidence. I prefer something along the lines of "It was a pleasure to meet you yesterday."
- Follow that up with a few particulars regarding things you enjoyed hearing or learning from them about the position, the firm or the industry as a whole. As noted, please include particulars. Not, "It was great to hear more about your work."
- Reference something specific that makes you stand out as a candidate. Don't go with the vague, "I think I'd be the best person for the job." Include specifics from your skill set or background experience.
- If you mentioned a person, a book, an article, etc, during the meeting that you felt they would find of interest, mention it again and provide hard copy or a link to it.
- If you made any promises regarding follow-up material you would send along, note that again and give a date by when they can expect to receive it.
- Close with something along the lines of, "I look forward to hearing from you."
- I prefer "Sincerely" to "Best" or any of its derivatives.
- Spell- and grammar-check it.
- Print it out and read it on paper before sending it. It's easier to catch dropped or repeated words when you see them in this format.

All of these efforts will help to ensure that you've done all you can to present your best self.

## SUMMING IT UP:

- Pick three attributes you'd like an H.R. rep to use to describe you after your interview and work to manifest those.

- Make sure you choose from a wide "tonal" palette: demonstrate a variety of coping styles for approaching deadlines, difficult coworkers, crucial conversations, etc.

- Have a specific answer to softball questions like, "Why should I hire you?" or "Why do you want to work for us?"

- Work out the worst three questions you might get asked and know the answers.

- Research the firm, the competition, the industry, exhaustively.

- Remain aware of your physicality at all times. It's easy to put others off with sloppy body language.

- If you can't fix a glitch in your résumé, skill set, background, try to find a way to talk about it as an asset.

- Setting up an informational interview can help you discover what employers want to hear—and what they never want to hear.

- Know and prioritize what you value in terms of autonomy, teamwork, benefits.

- Know your walk-away number. Be confident in the skills you offer.

- Recognize that financial negotiations are very rarely personal. Keep your equilibrium and, if possible, a sense of humor, throughout.

- Ensure your follow-up correspondence is prompt, professional, polished.

## CHAPTER FIVE

# Stand and Deliver:
## Giving Speeches That Bring People to Their Feet

The ancients said, "*When Cicero speaks, people say, 'What an intelligent man is Cicero.' When Demosthenes speaks, people say, 'Let us march.'*"

This, to me, is the speaking "ideal": to leave your listeners more than informed—to leave them inspired enough to join you on the barricades.

Is this easy to do? No. It takes work.

Can you do it? Yes. I promise you can.

For many people, speaking in public feels a lot like being thrown to the lions. Clients tell me their hands sweat, their hearts pound, sometimes their faces turn red . . . .

You know what? My hands sweat, my heart pounds, sometimes my face turns red . . . .

The trick in this moment is to tell yourself—and believe—that these are good things.

How can they be good? Because all of these signs are just manifestations of extra energy. And an energetic speaker is an interesting speaker.

They also mean that you care. If you didn't care, they wouldn't happen. And caring is key. Caring equals commitment. And commitment is what carries the day even if you forget half your points, spill your water, and trip as you leave the stage.

If you doubt this, think back for a minute to any school play you've attended. Were the performances Shakespearean? Were the costumes breathtaking? Did the special effects knock you out? Probably not. But were those kids *so* excited to be on that stage performing for you that none of these things mattered? I'm guessing, yes. I'm guessing you were clapping wildly along with the rest of the audience when they came out to take their bow.

So if it wasn't about the technical aspects of their performance, what were you responding to? Their commitment—their genuine enthusiasm for entertaining you. Commitment is the X factor, and this chapter's where you find it, along with all the other tools you'll need to be polished, informative, and delightful. The tools that will get your audience to, "Let us march!"

## Your Black Book for Speeches

From time to time it's been suggested that I might be the tiniest bit controlling. I prefer the word efficient or, if you must, directive. This quality stands me in good stead when I'm getting a client ready for a speech.

When my dream scenario occurs the client calls me early enough that I'm able to ask any number of questions that make up what comes to be known as "The Black Book." Those questions follow.

*Note:* While some of these questions may seem shockingly basic, you'd be surprised at how infrequently my clients know the answers. This is generally due to two factors: one, they didn't know the questions to ask; or two, someone in their marketing department has been taking care of it so they aren't aware of the details. If you are in the second group, make no mistake about it: the details are your concern. When the time comes to wow, you are the one who's going to be standing on that stage, not your assistant marketing executive.

- What is the venue for the speech?
- How large do you expect the audience to be?

- What is the general demographic makeup of the group? For example: students, mid-level management, upper echelon management, etc.
- Is it possible to get a list of those attending?
- Do you have a mandate for me? (For example: to inspire, to educate, to entertain.)
- What, if anything, has the audience been told about my talk? Has it been advertised or promoted with a particular theme or tagline?
- Is this part of an ongoing series/training process/etc?
- If so, who are those speakers and what have they spoken about?
- What's the time limit?
- Would you like me to answer questions at the end?
- Are there hosts/sponsors/volunteers/attendees I need to thank?

If the speech is taking place at a luncheon/dinner/awards ceremony, it's important to include the following questions:

- Where am I in the lineup?
- Will food be served or courses cleared while I'm speaking?
- Will attendees have been offered drinks or cocktails prior to the event?

These questions are important for gauging both the noise level and how hungry/tired/inebriated your audience might be, so that you can plan accordingly.

Questions about the physical space—stage, podium, chairs, etc—are covered in the Advance Recon essay that follows, but the above broad strokes must be addressed as well. The answers will form the backbone of the speech you're going to give—help you pace yourself and gauge your audience so you all leave feeling exhilarated.

# Advance Recon

In the military, sending in an advance guard to check the particulars of a physical situation—the landscape, the buildings, the natural and manmade resources available to you—is known as advance reconnaissance, or "advance recon." My request is that when you are booked to do a speaking engagement you do the same. You, or someone you trust, should go to the site ahead of time and check the physical setup far enough in advance to be able to request any changes you might want, or at least get mentally prepared for the things you can't change. If you can't do an on-site recon, do one by telephone.

What kinds of things should you be looking for?

- What's the size and shape of the room—square or rectangle?

This is important because speaking in a large rectangular room is something you'll need to mentally prepare for, as it can feel a lot like you're speaking in a bowling alley. Knowing this ahead of time will ensure you're ready to bolster your words with the extra physicality needed for them to reach the back of the room. It will also give you time to consider if you want to address the shape of the room in your opening remarks. For example by saying something like, "It's a long, long room. If those of you in the back can't hear me, please send up a flare." Not only does this make it everybody's problem, it makes the people in the back—who may have been feeling like the sad stepchildren—feel included.

You'll also want to sit in every corner of the room to see if there is anywhere you're partially blocked from the audience's view. Again, knowing this ahead of time will allow you to consider how you can best make those people feel included.

- How are the acoustics of the room?

Can you be heard from every corner? Will you need a microphone? What kind of microphone will it be, stationary or walking? Is it possible to request one that will allow you to walk around if that's something you'd like to do?

- Where will you be seated prior to speaking: on the stage or in the audience?

If you're on the stage, will you be behind a table or just waiting in a chair? These choices will affect your physicality while you wait. If you're at a table, you need to sit up and forward and keep your hands where the audience can see them. If you're in a chair, you need to refrain from giving your audience a crotch shot: keep your feet side by side on the floor.

If you're scheduled to wait in the audience, what's the pathway for getting you to the stage? If that flight plan doesn't have you walking on from stage left, can that be changed? This is important because we read from left to right. If you walk on from stage right, we don't like you as much.

- What kind of podium will there be?

How high is it? Please don't take anything less than a specific inch count as an answer. Yes, it's a drag for someone to have to go measure it, but it needs to be done. First: so that you can practice ahead of time with a podium that's the correct height and know whether you'll need your glasses to see your notes. Second: because if you're not tall and the podium is, you'll need to prepare for that contingency either by asking ahead of time for something lower, or by speaking about it once you're standing there. Also, is the podium made of wood or Plexiglas? If it's Plexiglas, you're going to need to be mentally prepared to be more physically exposed. (You might also need to be prepared to ask someone to Windex it ahead of time.)

- Will there be a teleprompter?

If so, do you want to use it? It's not mandatory. If you do, who will be in charge of inputting your remarks, and controlling the speed once you're speaking? FYI: An answer like "That guy over there," isn't enough. Be sure to find out and remember his name. Also: what's the drop-dead time for making changes to your script?

Again, while asking some of these questions may seem like you're being too particular, it's not because you expect to have things changed to your liking. More often than not, it's so you're prepared for what you are walking into, will have considered the choices within your control, and so, will be able to be your best self for your audience.

## "Check. One. Two. Check."

Aside from the hairbrush many of us have used as a microphone while singing along to our favorite song in our bedroom, few of us have a lot of experience with a mic. This generally leads to wild over- or under-familiarity with it when we're confronted with the real thing.

Those who tend toward over-familiarity will often bang on the head of it or blow into it to see if it's working, then wrench it around a few times to get it to their desired angle. All of these choices are hard on the eardrums, and usually the nerves, of your audience.

Those who tend toward unfamiliarity won't test its capabilities at all, much less think of adjusting its height or angle.

This can be maddening for an audience who might then be unable either to hear or see you.

So how should you work with a microphone? First, assume whoever set it up checked the levels. If you are unsure whether you can be heard, simply ask, "Can everyone hear me?" There's no need to blow or bang.

Second, if you need to adjust its height or angle, stand as you will be standing while you speak—don't bend down toward it—then hold it at its base and move it slowly and gently to the desired position. As for the best angle: point a microphone at your chin. Pointing it directly at your mouth will give your audience far too much information about what's happening there.

## What's the "Once upon a time"?

There's a reason all the fairy tales begin, "Once upon a time." Very few children enjoy getting a lecture. (Let's face it: "The Three Little Pigs" wouldn't have gotten off the ground if it began, "Today I'm going to tell you why you should build your house out of bricks instead of straw.") The thing is, though, very few adults do either. Most of us still enjoy a story.

My recommendation, then, whether you're trying to get your teenager to realize the dangers of drinking and driving or trying to get shareholders to buy your stock, is to begin with your version of "Once upon a time": the who/what/where/when.

The best example I can give of the above, sadly, comes from the experience of a colleague of mine named Madeline. From time to time, Madeline and I do pro-bono work with seventh- and eighth-grade public school students on their presentation skills. Each semester, one class would begin with Madeline giving the opening to the following speech: "When I was nine, I woke up Christmas Eve morning to find my mother sitting on the end of the bed. Her face was white. I asked her what was wrong and she said, 'Your brother won't be coming home for Christmas this year. He was killed by a drunk driver last night.'"

Each year, you could have heard a pin drop. She had their attention—and had it in a very different way than she would have if she'd begun with "Today I'm going to tell you why it's important not to drink and drive."

The best way to do this is to speak from your personal experience. If you don't have direct personal experience, I've found another way that works for my clients (and their audiences) is to begin by saying, "When I found out I was coming to speak to you today, the first thing I did was X" (I did some reading and found this statistic/story/ quote) and it surprised/intrigued/delighted me . . ." You get the idea. The story of your preparing for the speech has become the story, the "Once upon a time . . ."

One of my clients recently provided me with a terrific example of this. He had to present Florida's Minister of Agriculture to a group made up of some native Floridians and some out-of-towners: all businesspeople. A businessman himself, he was stumped at first—what was the best way to make this person interesting to his audience? What could he say that would guarantee their attention? What was the "Once upon a time"?

The answer? He began with, "When I was asked to make this toast, I started thinking about the job of being Florida's Minister of Agriculture, and I realized I didn't know a lot about our agriculture, so I did some research. Did you know that twenty-five percent of the winter vegetables eaten in the *entire* United States are grown in Florida?" That was it: the once upon a time.

## "Opening amenities are opening inanities"

This is one of my favorite lines from Winston Churchill, although there are a lot from which to choose.

What does it mean? Most of us have been taught to begin our speeches the following way, "Good evening. My name is X. Thank you so much for being here tonight." Etc, etc.

These are amenities. These are niceties.

Why are they a problem?

As we've just learned, people love a story. Additionally, if people have come to hear you speak, they generally know who you are. Beginning in this way, then, means you have thrown away that first, crucial moment to appear to them as a master storyteller.

Secondly, we place more value on getting thanks from someone we know and admire. Thanking your audience before they've gotten the chance to know you means nothing to them. It will "read" for your audience as flattery, rather than sincerity.

Now I'm not saying thank-yous aren't important. I'm a big believer in the power of a well-placed thank-you. The key here is "well-placed." A better place to put your thank-yous is at the end of your speech. At that point, your thanks will mean more to them because they will feel like they know you, and because you will have entertained/

informed/inspired them they will like and respect you, which will make your thanks valuable to them. Additionally, they will have done something meriting a thank-you—they will have listened to you—so you will have a genuine reason to offer them your thanks.

Is this an easy way to begin your speech? Many people initially don't think so. Most of my clients have become so used to the, "Hi, I'm so-and-so/Thank you for coming" formula that leaving it out altogether gives them the jim-jams. When this occurs, I've found the easiest way around it is to videotape them doing it both ways. When we rewind and play it back they see how much stronger it is to begin with a story. If you're feeling the same way and have the option of taping yourself ahead of time, I recommend it strongly. You'll quickly see how much more compelling it is to open with a story.

## Ethos, Pathos, Logos

Sitting down to write a speech can be daunting. There are so many variables to consider—what you want to achieve, what your audience's interests are, etc—that it's easy to feel overwhelmed. One structure many people find helpful as they begin their work is to consider the three elements that Aristotle felt were integral to making an effective argument: ethos, pathos, and logos.

*Ethos/Ethics*: As your audience listens to you, some of the questions they'll have on their minds are: does this person have ethics? Is his reputation all it's cracked up to be? Is he worthy of my respect? Given that, you want to be sure these questions are answered. In some cases, your reputation will have preceded you—your authority will have been established by your title, advance promotion, or an introduction. Nevertheless, it's always helpful to include details that support the reputation you've earned, and demonstrate its integrity.

*Pathos/Empathy*: Other questions your audience will be asking themselves are: does this person have the ability to sympathize with me? Are his interests/life situation/values in line with mine? Does he care about what I care about? Does he understand my point of view?

Including stories, examples, and details that demonstrate similar life experiences and/or that you share their point of view will go a long way toward engaging them and, ultimately, having them root for you.

*Logos/Logic:* Finally, your audience needs to feel sure that your arguments are sound—based on statistics, facts, irrefutable reasoning. This is one arena where it's easy to leave out a step or two because you've been living inside the conclusion of your argument for so long that you forget the building blocks that went into arriving at that conclusion. For this reason, it's helpful to run your reasoning past a friend with no knowledge of the subject, but whom you know to be extremely logical. (I have two go-to people for these moments . . . logic isn't my strongest asset.) This is an easy way to ensure you haven't left any plot holes.

Ethos, pathos, logos . . . it's wonderful to me that these fundamental cornerstones, identified so long ago, are still so vitally important to the work we do today.

## The Rule of Three

Have you ever noticed that there are frequently three characters in stories? Three musketeers, three stooges, three pigs, three bears, three blind mice . . . not to mention that you always get three wishes.

There's a very good reason for this. It seems our brains like to think in threes. Add one more and we mentally drop the ball. (Do you think it's an accident that Ringo always falls by the wayside when people talk about the Beatles? And forget about the Marx Brothers. I mean, everybody gets Harpo, Groucho, Chico . . . and then? Gummo and Zeppo are simply bonus points in a trivia game.)

Knowing this "Rule of Three" is invaluable when you sit down to road map your story, your pitch, your letter. If you're feeling overwhelmed by how to structure the multitude of possible directions you might go in, pick the three stories or ideas that best illustrate your point. Then pick three examples or statistics that support each of these.

The beauty of this method is that in addition to making it easier to structure what you want to say, you make it easier for your audience to retain what you've said.

## "Nerves are the respect you pay your audience"

This is a line I loved in the movie *Being Julia*. In this film, Annette Bening plays an aging actress who was once the toast of London's theatrical world. "Nerves are the respect you pay your audience," is her advice to the ingenue who is longing to usurp her position. I think it's a line that anyone getting ready to speak to a group can find beneficial.

Why? Because being nervous is a plus. As I've mentioned, the clients who make me the most nervous are the ones who aren't nervous. I think the trick to managing nervousness is starting to think of being nervous simply as being alive.

Here's an example of what I mean. When I quit my job in publishing to do freelance work, one of my psych authors took me out to lunch and gave me the best advice I've ever received about running your own shop. She said, "You're always going to be anxious, because you'll never have the 'right' amount of work. You'll usually have way too much or way too little. The trick is not to label feeling anxious as bad. The trick is to say to yourself, 'Oh, I'm anxious. I must be alive.' Because the perception that anxiety is bad is only going to make you more anxious."

The same is true for nervousness. Once you've labeled it as bad, you naturally begin to want to rid yourself of it. This generally backfires in one of two ways: You either do such a good job that you come across to your audience as lifeless, or you work so hard to manage your nervousness that you aren't present for your speech and so, are unable to be your best self. Stuffing down nervousness is a lose-lose.

What can you do instead? I recommend you say to yourself, "Wow, I'm nervous. Excellent! That means I'm alive and have energy to spare. What should I do with this spare energy? Give it away—knock the socks off my audience."

As you learn to do this—to welcome nervousness, breathe into it, and recycle it as additional commitment and animation—you may actually begin to look forward to it, to try to be nervous if you aren't nervous. Which, of course, is good, because you've started the cycle once again.

## Making an Entrance

When I was growing up there was a perfume ad whose tagline was "Make an Entrance Without Saying a Word." While I no longer remember which perfume it was advertising, I do remember the sentiment every time I see someone heading up to a podium, or walking onto a stage. The speaker who scuttles toward the stage, who is mesmerized by his feet as he heads toward the stage, who is rearranging his notes as he walks toward the stage, etc, does not inspire me with confidence. Instead, sympathy pains kick in— I begin to get nervous for them, or feel faint tremors of trepidation for myself.

What would I prefer instead? NASA claims that 50 percent of a rocket's fuel is used to go the first mile. I find this a fascinating percentage. This is the spirit in which I'd like you to launch yourself toward the stage—as if you can't wait to get up there and begin inspiring, persuading, entertaining me.

And, to continue the rocket analogy, I'd like your energy used

### It's a Runway, Not a Roadway

Every now and then I have a client ask me what I think about their taking some kind of medication to help their nerves before they give their speech. While this isn't something on which I'm qualified to give advice, it is something about which I have an opinion. And that opinion is that I would prefer that they didn't. I think there's a lot of value to be gained in learning to manage nervousness effectively—both in the immediate situation, and as they move through their life.

That said, if you truly find your nervousness incapacitating then, by all means, speak with someone authorized to prescribe something about prescribing something. My request, however, is that you think of it as a runway not a roadway—let it get you off the ground in this moment, but don't rely on it for the journey. I'd like you to think of it as a temporary solution as you work toward trusting your talent.

solely for this launch toward the stage. As mentioned, this is not the time to begin rearranging your notes—or your hair. I'm an F. Scott Fitzgerald junkie and one of the many moments I remember being struck by in *Tender Is the Night* is the analysis by the main characters of the various men who enter the restaurant where they are lunching. The premise is that no one has the sangfroid of the main character, Dick Diver, and it turns out nobody does. Each man, as he enters the room and feels the eyes of the group on him, feels compelled to touch his hair, adjust his tie, smooth down his coat. In other words, they begin to fidget. Don't fidget. Instead, use this nervous energy for point three:

Smile. Again, this feels like something so basic it doesn't need to be mentioned, but it does. Whether because we're nervous, and so forget, or because we think it projects the wrong impression—makes us seem less authoritative or serious—we neglect to smile. Now I'm not saying it's appropriate to smile when giving the statistics of the number of people who lost their homes or their lives in a recent natural disaster. I am, however, saying that it's important to smile in most situations. I'm not asking for the grin of the stand-up comedian of the moment, just an indication that you're pleased to see your audience.

I promise this will go a long way toward their being pleased to see you.

## Come Out! Come Out!

When we think of giving a speech, we generally think of ourselves delivering it while standing behind a podium. I'm going to ask you to consider coming out from behind that podium.

This is important because, as discussed, 55 percent of your impact comes from what your body is doing while you are speaking, and if the majority of your body is hidden from your audience you've lost an awful lot of your impact.

A great example of a person's body immeasurably enhancing their impact can be seen in the 1992 town hall meeting between Bill

Clinton and George H.W. Bush. Many of you will remember the phrase he used while speaking with a member of the audience: "I feel your pain." I believe the reason so many of us remember that is because of Mr. Clinton's physicality while saying it. If you were to look at it again, you would see he stepped toward the person with whom he was speaking, lifting his arm as if to touch him while he did so. By reinforcing his message with his body language his sincerity became palpable.

"Well," you may be thinking, "that's all very well for Mr. Clinton, but it's possible he's had a tad more experience in situations of this kind than I have. I need the podium." Okay, I am willing to concede he's had more public speaking experience than most Americans, but I stand firm in thinking the podium is far more of a hindrance than a help.

How, then, can you begin to think about working without a podium? The most important element is to make the jump from reading verbatim from a script, to having a list of bullet points with key words and/or concepts that serve as a road map for the journey you've prepared for your audience. The particulars for making this switch can be found in Chapter Seven, "Put It in Writing," but the heart of that essay—that this jump will do wonders for both your confidence and your audience's enjoyment—is worth saying again. By necessity, reading to an audience means you cannot have eye contact with them. Additionally, as stated, it means you remain trapped behind the podium. Finally, the act of reading and re-reading any script in preparation means that it's unlikely it will sound fresh when the time comes to give your speech. In other words, you'll be compromising both your physicality and your tonal quality.

Once you have your bullet points in-hand, I recommend placing them on the podium while you stand next to it. This strategy allows you to remain visible to your audience, but also keeps your map handy should you need to refer to it. For the record, this is how I speak. Then, when I need to check where I'm going, I simply step over and check my list. If I notice I've forgotten a point I want to make, I say, "Oh, one thing I forgot to mention when I was talking about X was," tell them, and move on. No one's ever complained about this (or, if they have, they haven't complained to me).

If this sounds overwhelming then, by all means, don't open with it. Do a few speeches from behind the podium and work up to it. A great way to practice working toward it is to come out from behind the podium during the question-and-answer part of the programming. This is a time when notes won't help you, and when your audience will appreciate the physical reinforcement of your accessibility.

## There's Nothing Neutral about Neutral

As anyone who's driven a standard car knows, neutral is the still center of the whirling cosmos of the gear shift—the place from which you transfer from first to third, from fourth to second, depending on the changing landscape of your fellow drivers, the posted speed limit, and the terrain you're negotiating.

In the world of acting and public speaking, standing in neutral provides the same function. It's the centered place from which you can easily move in any direction, depending on your needs, the needs of your audience, or the confines of the space you're in.

What does standing in neutral look like?

When you're standing in neutral, you're standing with your weight evenly on both feet and with your hands hanging by your sides.

Sounds simple, right?

Whether it does or doesn't, please read on. But before you do—if you're reading this while sitting down, get up and stand in neutral. Keep standing. Don't fidget. Don't shift your weight onto one foot or the other. Don't cross your arms in front of your chest or behind your back.

I'm guessing it's harder than it sounded.

In fact, standing in neutral takes practice for most people. Crossing our arms in front of our chests, or interlacing our fingers in front of our groins, is programmed into us on a cellular level. It's an instinctive gesture to protect our genitalia.

Now before you scoff—either because you don't believe me or because the use of the world genitalia bummed you out—think back to the disastrous choice made at the Oscars a few years ago when they had all the nominees come to the stage and stand in a line, then announced the winner. It was desperately uncomfortable to watch, yes?

Now I'll agree that part of the reason for that was because it was hideous for the losers to have to slink offstage after not receiving the award; but it was also because, by my utterly unscientific count, 95 percent of the people who came up there to stand laced their fingers together in front of their groins. It was like looking at a bunch of guys in a soccer goal. It drove me wild.

And it's precisely for this reason that standing in neutral is powerful. It "reads" for an audience on a visceral level as "He's so in command of himself that he doesn't need that protection."

Where can you look for some great examples of people standing in neutral? Peter O'Toole's got it down in *The Last Emperor*. Helen Mirren has said it's one of the reasons Jane Tennison, her character on *Prime Suspect*, is perceived as so powerful. And, regardless of what you may think about his politics, Bill Clinton is a master. His ability to stand in neutral brings me great joy.

The other important asset of neutral is that, as mentioned, it gives you the freedom to respond to changing energy needs within your presentation; for example, if you first need to persuade, then, to inspire, you need access to two very different kinds of physicality. It gives you options for handling feedback you're getting from your nerves; for example, spreading your fingers as wide as you can releases a lot of tension, as does exhaling to the full extent of your lung capacity—both of which are impossible to do with crossed arms or interlaced fingers. And, finally, it opens up the options you have for engaging in dialogue with your audience; for example, you can choose to come out from behind the podium or step toward people as they ask you questions.

So as you can see, neutral is powerful. If you can make a practice of trying to stand this way for just a few minutes a day, it will slowly become a habit that will stand you in good stead on any occasion.

## Nothing Beats Human

One of the most frequent misconceptions I run into is that a speech will be good if it's "perfect." If we dazzle our audience with our smarts and our charisma. If we knock them out with our authority and command of the material.

I'm here to tell you it's not true. Perfect isn't that interesting to watch. In fact, it can be both boring and exhausting. What we like to see is human. Here's what I mean by this:

One of my first clients was severely hampered by this idea of perfection. For him it translated as being very touch-me-not, very "just the facts, ma'am." This wasn't great anytime, but it really gummed up the works when he had to give an in-depth speech in a formal setting on improving relations between neighboring nations.

Our initial practices were tough. His face and voice were expressionless and he had a death grip on the podium, so I stopped him. "Tell me about a neighbor that you have." "What?" "Tell me about an actual neighbor that you have." At that, he launched into the most marvelous story about his eighty-five-year-old neighbor of thirty years—her feistiness and zest for life. As he spoke, his whole persona changed: his face lit up, his eyes danced, he released his grip on the podium.

These are the moments when I'm grateful for my video camera. I rewound the tape and had him watch the two segments: first his formal, "perfect" speech, then his delightful, impromptu one. As he watched, he saw the difference: the warmth and respect he had for this woman was so much more compelling to look at than his freeze-dried facts and figures. But what to do? How could we incorporate that humanity into the topic he had to tackle?

What we did was to write the name of his neighbor into the margin of his speech every time the word "neighbor" was mentioned.

This helped him stay connected to the "human factor" in the word neighbor, and to his own very human feelings about his actual neighbor. After that we found human associations for other dry words and concepts he had to include. These margin notes throughout helped him to stay connected in a heartfelt way to the material he had to cover. The upshot? He had the audience eating out of the palm of his hand, delighted by both his humanity and his ability to make broad concepts feel accessible and immediate.

So the next time you're faced with having to give a talk that's heavy on abstract concepts, statistics, work-related procedural information—anything you're finding it hard to connect to—I recommend taking the time to find a comparable trigger from your life that helps you connect to a very human emotion, then write that word or phrase in the margin. You'll be amazed at how this will transform the information for your audience, and you in their eyes.

## Pumpkin/Raisin

This is another exercise that came to me courtesy of my acting chums. Interestingly, but not surprisingly, the models with whom I work also have it in their toolbox. It's the "pumpkin/raisin" exercise.

How do you do it? It's simple enough. First, you make your face as big as a jack o' lantern: stretch your mouth into an enormous grin, open your eyes as wide as you possibly can, stick out your tongue as far as you possibly can. Next, you make your face as small as a raisin: purse your mouth as tightly as you can, squeeze your eyes closed, suck your cheeks in, furrow your brow. Then, become a pumpkin again, then a raisin, then a pumpkin, then a raisin . . . you get the idea.

Why would you do this? Well, you have forty-four muscles in your face, and only four of them are used for chewing. Most of the time, however, those are the muscles getting the biggest workout. We use a few more to yickety yak, but day to day the muscles controlling our potential range of facial expressions rarely get used. Additionally, in the same way the other muscles in our body get tense when we're nervous, the muscles in our face get tense when we're nervous, limiting our potential expressiveness even further.

The thing is, though, that in the same way varying your tonal quality makes your voice more interesting to listen to, broadening the scope of your facial expression makes your face more interesting to look at. And, when you're speaking to a crowd, you want to use every tool you can to be sure you have all eyes on you.

(This means that if you're someone who's a fan of Botox, it's worth getting it done *well*. Once we can no longer see your face moving, your message is automatically less interesting. In fact, the conversation afterward is often about how your face wasn't moving, as opposed to the point you were trying to make.)

Do some of my clients at first feel silly doing this exercise? Yes. Do many of them initially resent it, and me, enormously for making them do this exercise? You bet. But when they look at themselves in a mirror, or on videotape, after doing it, they see the difference immediately. Their faces are more alive, more expressive, more interesting. The words they are saying—the same words we've been practicing all along—seem more important. They get it.

All of which is, to me, worth a few moments of feeling silly.

## Solvitor Ambulando

As you may have noticed, I have a wide cast of characters from whom I draw inspiration. Among them is St. Augustine, one of the most influential saints in Western Christianity. One of the things he is said to have believed, that I happen to love and agree with, is *Solvitor ambulando*: It is solved by walking.

What does this mean? Well, have you ever noticed how many truly unnecessary fights occur when you're trapped in a car or across the table in a restaurant with someone? My personal theory is that this is because people aren't able to move around—to give their feelings a physical outlet—and as these feelings get throttled by the small space, the possibilities for problem-solving are choked off.

Perhaps this is the reason people say they need to "walk it off" when they want to cool off about something.

How can walking help you with speeches?

Clients often call me when they don't know exactly what they want to say, to ask me if I can figure it out for them. "No," I tell them, "but I can help you figure it out. Let's go for a walk."

Many people get cranky at this. Many people think I'm stalling.

But what I've discovered, and what they discover by the end of the walk, is that they do know what they think, or feel, or want to say, but that these thoughts and feelings haven't had room to grow because they've been trying to problem-solve while sitting in chairs, behind desks, or at keyboards. Moving around helps them find the emotional impulses behind what they're thinking, so the ideas come. It also helps them find the cadence they need to express their thoughts eloquently.

If you're feeling a little skeptical at this point, consider that Wallace Stevens, one of America's foremost poets and two-time winner of the National Book Award, worked as an insurance salesman throughout his life. When did he write his poetry? Walking back and forth to his insurance office every day. He says that it was during those times that the words and the rhythms would come to him. Then, when he got to his desk or his home, he would write them down.

Another thing that walking and talking your speech out loud does is to help you to embed the final product in your body, which helps with retention, and to notice how and when you plan to transition from one idea to another. Someone who used to put this into practice, though with swimming not walking, was Frank Sinatra. When he was working on a new song, he would "practice it" while swimming—use that time to embed it in his body and coordinate it with his breathing. Personally, I think this is one of the things that made him a star. He truly was singing from his heart; the heart that had worked so hard to swim those laps.

Another great example of how embedding knowledge in the body helps the brain to retain it can be found in many kindergarten classrooms. Here, one of the ways teachers work with children who are having trouble learning the alphabet, is to have them draw the letters in wet sand or clay. The practice of learning with their muscles as well as with their minds helps them to retain this information more easily.

So the next time you are having an unnecessary fight, writer's block, or stage fright, get up and move yourself around. I'm convinced that if psychoanalysts opened "talk therapy" up to "walk and talk therapy" they'd solve twice the problems in half the time.

## Make It Everybody's Problem

When you're preparing for a speech, it can be easy to think of all the things that can go wrong: you'll forget your talking points, you'll spill your water, your technology will go down. . . . As we've been known to say at my house, "Add another worry to the worry hopper." Some of this worry can be useful; it can force you to consider what you will do if that contingency arises. The trouble, however, is that you can never have complete control over every aspect or element of your presentation. You might still forget your talking points. You might still spill your water. Your tech might still go down.

What can you do if this happens?

The best advice I can give you is to make it everybody's problem—acknowledge it in an unflustered fashion and move on: "Hang on, my mind just went blank." "There goes the water." "As you can see, we're having a tech issue," etc. Attempting to cover up what's occurred is far more uncomfortable for your audience. After all, they can generally see what's happened. For you to pretend it didn't puts a big, fat elephant in the room. Acknowledging it, however, makes you coconspirators. It invites the audience to be on your side. It also keeps your mind free to move forward with what you've been talking about. You don't have to divert attention and energy to trying to cover it up.

Another default I often see in these moments is the profuse apology. A speaker rubs up against being human (forgetting something, spilling something) or an act of God (which is how I feel about tech breakdown) and, out of nervousness, apologizes for it again and again. Know this: one "I'm sorry" is okay; repeated apologies simply serve to keep our attention on what happened.

Making it everybody's problem is also important to keep in mind prior to your speech should you find yourself uncomfortable with the temperature of the room, the height of the podium, the location of your seat, etc. Too often, we don't want to say anything because we don't want to come across as difficult, or pushy. The trouble with this is that not saying anything generally doesn't stop you from thinking about it, which means you can't be fully present for the speech you're going to give, or the questions you're about to answer. A portion of your brain will be occupied thinking about how hot or uncomfortable you are. Articulating the situation—even if it can't be fixed—frees you to focus on the most important item on the agenda: doing your best work.

## Stick Your Landing

We've all seen Olympic gymnasts who dazzle with their routine but lose critical points with a hop or a stumble or a full blown sit down on their landing—at that point it doesn't matter if they've completed a triple handspring combination with a final half-twisting somersault, they've damaged the impression they've made. The same applies to speaking—all the flourishes and fancy footwork you included in your speech must be grounded by your finish, or you'll leave your audience disappointed. You need to stick your landing.

How can you ensure this? There are two factors in play. One is the advance preparation you will do, and the other is the advance practice you will do. Preparation guarantees you know where and how you will be landing, and practice ensures you have the stamina to get there—because it doesn't matter how good your closing is if you lose your energy and focus before arriving.

Charles Osgood, in his book *Osgood on Speaking*, tells his readers that when he is working on his television scripts he writes his last sentence first. This keeps him focused on what he wants to leave readers with when the segment is over. This concept makes sense to me. In the same way you probably don't get into your car or onto an airplane without a clear idea of where you're headed, you don't want to give a speech without a clear idea of where you want to take your audience. Once that's established, the route you use to get there can shift according to circumstance, but both passengers and driver are more comfortable knowing a destination has been chosen.

With that in hand, it's time to look at stamina—making sure you tackle the end of your speech with the same conviction and focus you had when you began. This can be tricky for a couple of reasons. Sometimes because beginning is so difficult that that's where our pre-speech energy got spent: where we'll stand, how we'll stand, what we'll say, sucked up a lot of prep time. Sometimes because we're so anxious to get there that we rush toward our conclusion—the sooner we finish, the sooner we get to sit down.

But pilots practice both takeoffs and landings, and car accidents usually happen within two miles of home. You can't rush your finish.

This is why practicing out loud is so critical. You will hear, or your trusted colleague or family member will hear, when you've begun to career toward your finish, and you can adjust accordingly.

Finally, in the same way the gymnast salutes the crowd, arms raised in victory, regardless of how the routine went, you need to stand and acknowledge your audience's applause, regardless of how you might feel your speech went. Not doing so is disrespectful to the effort both you, and they, expended.

## Plant the Question

A common mistake I see is for a speaker to finish strongly, and then undermine all the good work he's done by asking, "Does anyone have any questions?"

Why is this a problem? Because if no one has a question, or no one wants to speak first, it's the ultimate awkward silence. The speaker gets embarrassed, and the audience is suddenly riddled with guilt, or left to wonder why—if they thought the speaker was so good—he wasn't more thought-provoking.

How can you set yourself up so that this doesn't happen? One way is to include the phrase, "I will be leaving time for questions at the end" at the beginning. This provides your listeners with a heads-up to be listening with a questioning mindset. The other way is to have planted a conversation-provoking question in the audience with a colleague or friend. Make it their job to have their hand in the air seconds after you've asked, "Does anybody have any questions?" This is often all that's needed to get the ball rolling. People feel less awkward because they aren't going first, and because you will, of course, have demonstrated your complete affability and willingness to tackle questions from the floor.

If, heaven forfend, you forget to plant a question in the audience ahead of time, and you ask, "Does anyone have any questions?" only to have it fall into dead silence, there is a way to save the situation. Your go-to phrase in that moment is, "A question I'm often asked is X." Then, you give the answer to that question. This technique is useful because it will often trigger ideas for your audience members, or—if it's a question they've all been wondering about but been too shy or anxious or lethargic to ask—your willingness to talk about it will help to open things up.

And even if that doesn't happen, you will have gracefully gotten yourself off the hook.

## Mired in Minutiae

It's almost inevitable that one question in your question-and-answer session will be rooted very deeply in the particulars of that questioner's situation. For example, the subject under discussion is refinancing your mortgage, and your questioner will stand up and treat everyone to the ins and outs of their relationship to the person from whom they bought the house, the condition the house is currently in, how this differs from the condition the house was in when they bought it, their feelings about the sorry state of the economy today, etc, etc . . . .

In these moments, it's important to redirect the question so your answer is user-friendly for all. The tricky bit is doing this in such a way that you don't offend or shame the questioner, while reassuring the audience that you're aware they've begun shifting in their seats. My best advice is to handle it as follows:

- "I'm going to interrupt you." Not, "May I interrupt you?" which rarely slows the flow of commentary and doesn't convince the audience you're still in charge.
- "I think the question you're asking has a broader context." This reassures your questioner that his question is important.
- "That context is X, Y, Z." At this point you reframe the question so it does, in fact, have a broader context.
- "My answer to that question is P, D, Q." Here, you answer the question you have asked.
- "If you still have questions about the particulars of your situation, feel free to catch me at the end of the session." This allows you to both validate your questioner's concerns and move the conversation along.

Should your questioner persist, you can follow with,

- "Unfortunately, it's not feasible for me to speak to the individual concerns of each audience member. As I said, I'm happy to speak with you privately if there's time at the end of the session."

But if you're going to use happy, be sure to sound happy—or at least neutral.

## The Art of the Introduction

Introducing others often seems so inconsequential compared to having to give a speech that the work required to do it elegantly and effectively is forgotten. It's only when we are standing up in front of the room searching for the words we need, while looking at the upcoming speaker's expectant face, that we realize there's an art to the introduction.

When you are asked to introduce someone, the first thing you need to do—if it isn't immediately apparent—is to ask the person who's asked you to do the introduction why they wanted to hear that particular speaker. What is it about the speaker's background or experience or expertise that was compelling to them, and will (hopefully) be compelling to the audience? Next, you need to call up the person whom you are introducing and ask him or her if there is anything in particular they would like you to say: do they want you to provide a "tease" for what they will be talking about? Do they want you to list their credentials? And, just as importantly, is there anything they *don't* want you to mention about their information or background or credentials?

Additionally, if they're willing—and have prepared them ahead of time—you should ask to see a draft or outline or bullet points on what they will be talking about. The reason for this is not to steal their thunder by telling the audience what they are going to tell them (my idea of hell) but to see if there is a piece of what they are going to talk about that is particularly interesting to, or resonant for, you. This is often an easy and effective way to dive into personalizing the introduction for yourself—to begin building a story for your audience. It's a tactic that releases you from the sad and tired, "Tonight I have the pleasure of presenting the distinguished Mr. X whom I know we all can't wait to hear talk about Y." Instead you have the option of, "When I found out I was going to get to introduce Mr. X, I was so pleased because I also have a small business/a sullen teenager/a fear of heights"—whatever common ground you may have discovered—"myself, as many of you do, and I've always wanted to hear how he was able to do Y."

Now that you've gotten a handle on the words you are going to say, you can begin to think about the tonality and physicality of your introduction. As always, if you say you are so pleased, or happy, or excited to be introducing someone, then I want your voice and your face to look pleased or happy or excited. Physically, I want you to gesture toward the speaker when you say his or her name. It always strikes me as so odd-looking when this isn't done—someone's standing up doing a big yickety yak about a person without ever physically referencing them, leaving the audience craning their necks trying to figure out who on earth is being talked about. Gesturing toward the speaker gives the audience an opportunity to visually flag the person for themselves. When you've finished what you want to say, I want you to begin to lead the applause, which will trigger the audience to begin applauding as well. This important piece is often overlooked, which generally results in tentative, anemic opening applause—not a great confidence-builder for speaker or audience. Finally, when the speaker gets to the stage, I want you to shake hands or kiss or embrace him or her (that's your choice) and then physically move them in front of you toward the podium, while you walk behind them back to your seat. This will avoid the awkward do-si-do that can occur when no one is definitive about the flight pattern.

Though it can seem like overkill to put this much thought into something so seemingly small, I can promise you that if you do you will be able to take your seat feeling confident that you did everything in your power to set up both the speaker and the audience for an enjoyable speech to come.

## *Gloat* Back to Your Seat

In the same way it's important to pause and collect the room before
you begin to speak, it's important to manage your physicality while
you *return* to your seat.

As many of you know, sometimes you listen to the speaker, and
sometimes you don't—sometimes your mind returns to whatever
problem it's currently working over like a chew-toy: "I wonder what
my boss meant by that?" "Why does X always have to have his own
way?" "Why can't Y take over some of the filing?"

Suddenly, everyone around you is clapping. You realize your
speaker's wrapped up. Newly focused on him, you notice that he's
walking back to his seat kind of furtively. His head is down, his
shoulders are slumped . . . "Hmmm," you think, "I guess it's not
my fault I stopped listening. He must have been worse than I
thought . . . ."

Here's the thing. For any number of reasons outside your control,
it's possible some members of your audience won't be hanging on
every word you say. We all have a lot going on in our lives, and sometimes even the best speakers have an off day. It's still possible, however, regardless of how well you've done or your audience has
listened, to influence your audience's perception of your performance by how you return to your seat.

How do you do this? Give them your biggest smile while you're
still at the podium. Remain standing there while people are applauding. As much as you think you may not deserve it, they may not feel
the same. In the same way that giving someone a compliment that
they shrug off can hurt your feelings, not acknowledging your audience's appreciation can hurt theirs. Gather up any notes or papers
you may have with you unhurriedly. Then, shoulders back, head up,
unflustered—still with your big smile—return to your seat. Note: Do
*not* immediately begin debriefing with your companions about forgetting bullet point three on page four. Any mistakes you may have
made can go to the grave with you.

Leaving the podium in this way leaves an impression of pleasure in your own performance, which your audience will accept at face value. If you need to go into the bathroom later and lose your mind, be my guest—but please gloat back to your seat.

## SUMMING IT UP:

- Learn everything you can about the intention for the evening and the way your speech has been billed to others prior to beginning to write.

- Perform a full advance reconnaissance on the physical space before arriving. No detail is too small.

- Speechwriting is storytelling. Begin with the "Once upon a time . . . ."

- Opening with who you are/thanks for coming is expected and so just white noise for your audience. Don't do it.

- Ethos, pathos, and logos—ethics, empathy, and logic—are integral to capturing your listener's hearts and minds.

- Try to avoid labeling feeling nervous as "bad." Shift to, "Nervous is terrific—it means I'm alive, and I care about what I'm presenting."

- Launch yourself out of your chair. Refrain from fidgeting when you arrive at the podium. Smile.

- Physically reinforce your accessibility to your audience by coming out from behind the podium whenever possible.

- Standing in neutral is a position of strength. Practice it.

- Demonstrating your humanity to your audience will engage them far more than striving for perfection.

- Warming up your face before speaking is as important as warming up your body before you begin playing a sport.

- If you are stuck while writing, or inhibited by the idea of presenting, try walking it through as well as talking it through.

- If there's a glitch, don't attempt to suppress or ignore it. Acknowledge it and move on.

- Consider writing your last sentence first, so you can be certain where you are headed. Make sure you leave yourself enough energy to get there.

- If you plan to include question and answer as part of your presentation, make sure you have planted a question in the audience beforehand.

- Redirect a question mired in a questioner's personal minutiae with, "I think your question has a broader context."

- Introducing others is a presentation. Don't be fooled into thinking that the amount of preparation is congruous with the length of a presentation.

- No matter how you feel you did, gloat back to your seat.

## CHAPTER SIX

# Pointed PowerPoint:
## Making PowerPoint Powerful

I love PowerPoint. I love it!

That said, I rarely love PowerPoint Presentations, and I'm guessing I'm not alone when I say this.

As you know, PowerPoint is an amazing tool. If you are making a presentation that will be enhanced by visuals, having PowerPoint at your disposal makes your presentation far more effective.

The trouble is, a lot of us forget that the important word in that sentence is *enhanced*. In the same way money gets a bad rap when people focus on money being the problem in the phrase "The love of money is the root of all evil"—not noticing the "love of" portion of the programming—PowerPoint gets a bad rap when we forget it's there to *enhance* our presentation, not *be* our presentation. You are always the presentation, not your visuals. In my ideal world, next to nothing coming out of your mouth is replicated on the slides you include. If there is crossover, it's only to aid your audience in jotting down hard facts or figures if their pens, or typing, are moving more slowly than your speech.

Consequently, this section will look at how you can put together effective visuals that don't overshadow or detract from, but instead enhance, you—the main event.

## Practice Is Perfect

While PowerPoint can make life easier in many ways, and often does, one of the drawbacks to using it is that we get so caught up in building our deck that we don't have the stamina left over to practice the presentation of that deck. We get deck fatigue.

Alternatively, some of us have come to think that because we have the visuals we no longer have to be concerned about how we are going to present those visuals.

And, finally, many of us feel stupid practicing out loud when there's no audience present. It feels too much like being back in kindergarten playing make-believe—and I get that. For the record, I hated make-believe. I am what nursery school teachers refer to as "very grounded in reality."

That said, I can't say often enough how important it is to practice every presentation out loud before you deliver it—and particularly your PowerPoint presentations. It's too easy to succumb to the idea that having visual aids is enough to make an impact.

Finally—and I don't imagine there are very many of you who are going to like reading this—it's not enough to practice it once and say, "Okay. I see what I need to do. I don't need to practice it again." You need to practice it again. And then you need to practice it at least once more after that.

Knowing the dismay this may strike into many hearts, I plundered my quote file for quotes about the importance of practice in the hope that these will provide you with the inspiration you, or your team, might need to get your presentation on its feet again and again. Here they are:

"Practice is the best of all instructors."
*Publius Syrus*

"People seldom see the halting and painful steps by which the most insignificant success is achieved."
*Annie Sullivan*

"Practice is a means of inviting the perfection desired."
*Martha Graham*

"The secret of success is to be ready when your opportunity comes."
*Benjamin Disraeli*

"Each man has an aptitude born with him. Do your work."
*Ralph Waldo Emerson*

## Batter Up!

From time to time you'll find yourself giving the same presentation more than once—and, if you're training sales staff, seeking investors, or informing board members, a lot more than once. At these times it can be hard to get it up to do it one more time. With feeling.

A great way to combat this is to think of yourself as the key player on your favorite sports team who, you can be sure, doesn't go out on the field or the court or the ice thinking, "Here we go again . . . one more game." In the same way the rules remain the same but the game is entirely different each time it's played, your presentation will contain the same slides but the game itself will be different each time you play it. And every time you face off against a different opposing team, in a different conference room, in a different climate, you will need to adjust your game to those new conditions.

## Ready, Set, Room

When your presentation is being given as a slideshow, all the room factors covered in the Advance Recon essay in the speech-giving chapter should be addressed: What's the size and shape of the room? What's the sound quality? Where is the table? Where do you want to be in relation to the table? Is the microphone attached to the podium or will you have a walking mic? How high is the podium? Etc, etc.

Additionally, here are some very specific, but meaningful, ways you can make the room's logistics work in your favor:

- *Most important*, you need to ensure that the podium or table from behind which you are speaking is at the left of the screen as the audience faces you. Why? Because we read from left to right, and if you stand to the right of the screen you're making us work too hard to read your slides; this means we don't like you as much.

- If you have someone running your technology, you need to make sure he or she is in your sightline (preferably directly across the room from you) because, should the technology go down, you don't want to have to turn your back to the audience to handle the problem.
- Should you have to point to something on the screen, you will do so only with your left hand, without turning your back to the audience. (Yes, you do want to channel your inner Vanna White.)
- Make sure you have a light source that will light you once the room is darkened. It's a lot harder to shine when your audience can't see you. If you present a lot in different conference rooms and so aren't ever sure what you'll be walking into, it's worth investing in a small spotlight (available at RadioShack) to bring with you when you speak.
- Have the person who turns down the lights when the slides begin know to turn them up again during your question-and-answer session. Q & A is tough enough without doing it in the dark.

While all of these elements might seem small by themselves, one by one, they add up. So it's worth a few phone calls to make sure you have everything that you can control under your control.

## Hit Your Numbers HARD

Many of my clients are bankers and so, immersed in numbers all day long. Now I don't believe that in this instance "familiarity breeds contempt," but it does often lend itself to a somewhat deadpan delivery when talking about the millions and billions.

My overarching advice in these moments is that they channel their inner Publishers Clearing House Sweepstakes voice: "Our net profits rose four point two MILLION dollars last year." "Our sales team beat its estimate by eight MILLION dollars," etc.

The same advice holds true for other industries as well. A phrase like "Our magazine has five million readers worldwide," is heard very differently than "Our magazine has FIVE MILLION readers worldwide."

You'll also want to be sure you're working your numbers to the limit when you're giving statistics. Contrast the following two statements:

"We're number six on the list of the top one hundred hotels in the world, which is impressive given we weren't even on the list in 2004."

"We're number six on the list of the top one hundred hotels in the country, which is impressive given we weren't even ON the list *just two years ago*."

You get the idea. Anytime you've got a number in your presentation, underline it, put it in all caps, make it bold . . . do whatever it takes to remind you that it's an opportunity.

## A List Is a Party

In contrast to today's world—where being on a list gets you into the party—when speaking in public, a list *is* the party.

What does this mean?

I'll give you an example. One day I was working with a client who was talking about fashion. She was saying a dress epitomized style, sophistication, and luxury. As she said these three adjectives her tonal quality didn't vary, however. Nothing "popped," nothing was memorable.

Now the fact is that style, sophistication, and luxury are three very different words with three very different meanings. And if you really want your listener to get that—and to stay with you while you're talking—you need to vary your tone as you say each word.

So we talked about how each word sounded, and what it signified, for her. Ultimately, we decided that "style" sounds short and sharp and bright, "sophistication" sounds strong, authoritative and elegant, and "luxury" wraps you in a cashmere blanket of sound: it's low and slow and growly. With these thoughts in mind, she repeated the description of the dress. Suddenly, it was far more interesting to listen to, and far more evocative of what she was describing.

So as you practice your presentation, or speech, or toast, should you have three adjectives side by side that you think you simply must use to make your point, take the time to break down how each word is different, and what each signifies for you. Then, use your tonal quality to amplify the distinctions between them.

Make your list a party.

## Margin Notes Are Anything but Marginal

As discussed, my preference when you're giving a PowerPoint presentation is that it's rare, if ever, that what you are saying is replicated on the slide on the screen. Given that, how do you prepare your presentation? Simple, but not easy. You create margin notes for yourself that trigger the necessary commentary for every slide.

Let me give you an example of what I mean by this. A new client called me to help him prepare a PowerPoint presentation for a real estate venture he was interested in finding backers for. When he arrived for our work together, his "presentation" was, essentially, him reading me the bullet points he had on the screen. Oh, no, my friend. Not okay.

During the course of our work we reconfigured his margin notes so that they worked as triggers for small stories he wanted to tell about each slide. When the slide with the land that had been set aside for community use was pictured, along with the square acreage it covered, his notes reminded him to talk about how families could use this green space to hike on Sunday afternoons. When the slide showing the land that had been set aside for community commerce came up, his notes said to talk about teenagers having a safe place to gather on "Main Street." When the slide detailing how much room there was between houses came up, his notes reminded him to talk about how this would allow families to individualize their homes—with swimming pools, room for their dog to run, jungle gyms for their kids, patios with barbeques, etc.

What these kinds of margin notes did was to make each slide come alive for the listeners. They could make a note of the square footage being discussed on each slide on their yellow legal pads, but at the same time they could imagine how they or their friends might use the space. This is what Benjamin Franklin referred to as "selling a ticket to treasure." This is when people buy in.

So the next time you sit down with your ideas for a PowerPoint presentation, make two lists for yourself: On one have the takeaway idea or statistic you want on each slide. On the other have the margin notes that will trigger the stories you are going to tell to make your presentation come alive.

## Setting Up Your Slides

In the same way how you say something, and what your body is doing while you say it, can significantly enhance or diminish your impact, how many slides you include in your PowerPoint presentation, how much text you include on each slide, and how you place the text on the slide, can significantly impact your audience's reaction to and retention of that information. Keeping the following rules and ideas in mind when you write up your slides will make a measurable difference in how your work is received:

- *The 10 20 30 Rule:* This is a rule created and espoused by Guy Kawasaki, Chief Evangelist of Apple Macintosh. He claims— and I agree—that every presentation should have no more than ten slides, should go on for no more than twenty minutes, and the type on each slide should be no smaller than thirty points. If you have to use smaller type to fit in all the things you want to say, then you don't have a strong handle on either how you factor into the presentation or on the material you're presenting.

- *The Reverse Six:* When placing multiple pieces of discrete information, logos, or pictures on one slide, you want to first sort the images by importance and then place them in a reverse six pattern on the slide, from most to least important. This will ensure the images you most want to highlight are in the slide's "sweet spot." [Note: you will see this same technique used to emphasize magazine cover taglines.]

- *The Left/Right Rule:* If you are placing two images or

### "You Can't Expect If You Don't Inspect"

Again, the above phrase comes courtesy of the Marine Corps where, as I understand it, it's often thrown around in connection with heavy artillery.

While I grant that the stakes in those moments are far higher, I think this aphorism is important to keep in mind as you head into your PowerPoint presentation. Too often we are so heavily reliant on our computers that we have no backup plan in mind should they fail. Additionally, we often neglect to call ahead to ensure our system is compatible with the technological setup of the situation we're walking into.

While I have no doubt that you have the charm and smarts to carry the presentation with no tech backup whatsoever, it would be a pity to have wasted all that time creating your presentation only to be unable to use it. So please inspect both your own equipment, and your host company's, ahead of time.

products side by side, you want to put the one you want your audience to choose, or pay greater attention to, on the right-hand side of the slide. No matter how sophisticated we may believe ourselves to be, we still view the left-hand side as sinister. (Note: this is why the majority of talk show hosts sit so they appear on the right-hand side of your television screen. It's also why when they do a product compare/contrast in a television commercial, the product they want you to buy will be on the right-hand side of your screen.)

As with so many things, the devil's in the details.

## Before, During, or After?

Many of us have gotten so used to having the question-and-answer part of a presentation come at the end of that presentation that it never occurs to us it can be done any other way. My feeling is that it can be done at least two other ways, and that there are advantages and disadvantages to all three choices. My recommendation regardless of what you choose, however, is to state your policy up front:

- "Before I begin, does anyone have any questions?"
- "Feel free to jump in if you have a question," or
- "I'm going to ask you to hold your questions until the end."

"Before I begin, does anyone have any questions?" can be helpful in moments when you sense tensions are brewing and people need to let off steam before they'll be able to listen to you. The downside to this choice is the possibility of getting so caught up in triaging the drama that you don't have adequate time left for your presentation.

The upside to giving people the green light to ask questions as they occur to them is that you forestall the possibility that someone will be so distracted by what they want to ask you that they find it impossible to listen to the remainder of your presentation. The potential downside is that you'll get distracted from your next point, or have that question and answer become an ongoing conversation. In the first case, don't apologize, but do take a moment to pause and think, "Hang on, I need a moment to collect my thoughts," should do it. If the second scenario occurs, don't hesitate to say, "I don't want to spend additional time on this at the moment. Let's plan to pick it up at the end."

And, finally, the upside to asking that questions be held until the end of the presentation is the elimination of the possibility of being distracted by questions, and the certainty that you have covered everything you wanted to cover. The downsides are the upsides listed above: that people will feel you're disconnected from their concerns, that they'll lose their focus, or that they'll lack adequate time to get their questions answered.

Ultimately, it comes down to the formality or informality of the occasion and personal choice. If the space you're in allows for people to jump in, and you're comfortable with that, questions before and/or during can help to keep both you and the audience energized. If it's not possible, set the stage for a vigorous final question and answer by planting the first question in the audience ahead of time, and coming around from behind the podium during the session as a physical reminder of your accessibility.

It bears repeating that if, at any time during question and answer, you lose your train of thought, don't hesitate to declare that and self-correct. "I just lost my train of thought—give me a moment," or "I'm afraid I lost my train of thought—can you repeat the question?" are both perfectly acceptable ways to get things back on track.

## It's Never a "Good Question"

This is a phrase that comes up a lot during the question-and-answer sessions following a presentation, and every time I hear it I get nervous.

Why? Because it's rarely heard as the speaker intends it.

In general, "Good question" comes out of a speaker's mouth in two moments: when he's been caught unprepared, or when he's been asked a question he doesn't want to answer. In that moment, he says "Good question" to fill the time while he's thinking.

The trouble with this is that he's now flagged his answer for the audience. They hear, "This is the one to listen to!"—when his intention was to do the opposite. Consequently, a question they might not have paid attention to before is now one they are sitting forward in their seats, waiting for the answer to.

The other drawback to saying "Good question" is that it makes everyone else who's asked a question feel theirs wasn't good, wasn't a thought-provoking crowd-pleaser.

Consequently, the only time I recommend using "Good question" is when you *really, really* want your audience to listen to your response. And even then, I'd rather hear you say, "I'm glad you asked me that."

## If a Picture's Worth a Thousand Words, How about a Prop?

We've all heard the phrase, "a picture is worth a thousand words." Given that, imagine how much you can say with a prop.

Let me give you an example: I had a client who was preparing a talk on high fructose corn syrup—HFCS—which is an ingredient in a lot of foods because it's cheaper than sugar, but which many people believe leads to higher blood triglycerides and raised insulin levels. When he came in, he had any number of slides detailing the ways HFCS is used in foods. In some foods, the ratio of glucose to sucrose was 50/50: some breads, crackers, condiments. In some it was as high as 90/10: some yogurts, cookies, sodas. It was all very scientific . . . and all very flat.

So I took him on a field trip to the grocery store where we picked up any number of items that I'm certain you think are healthy when you buy them (and which I'm not going to name because I'm not looking for a lawsuit), but which, in fact, are filled with HFCS. Bags and bags of low-fat salad dressings, ketchups, diet yogurts, diet sodas, pita breads, sandwich breads, peanut butters, crackers . . . Then, we arranged them on trays that we set up to run the length of the conference room table.

The next day when the group arrived, they had a field day. Everyone was picking things up, reading labels, passing things around to others, holding them up and exclaiming, "But I eat this because I thought it was good for me!" It became more than a presentation, it became a dynamic, interactive, memorable event. Everyone loved it. Everyone left talking about it. Everyone told my client he was a rock star.

So the next time you are putting together your presentation, consider whether there's a potential "show and tell" element that you can incorporate. Are there props that might enhance your visuals? Something you can include that everyone can easily and quickly pass around and/or interact with? Is there anything you can demonstrate yourself or ask someone to demonstrate for you? (My father told me the best speech he ever saw in college was one on rope rappelling. The guy ended it by rappelling out the window of the room—and not coming back. Apparently he got an A+.)

In every case, of course, my request is that the prop enhance your presentation, but not replace it, be gimmicky, or be so interactive that you lose your audience's attention. Choose carefully, then enjoy. Because when props work not only do they enhance your visuals, but their unexpectedness often brings a sense of freedom or play to the proceedings that your audience—which generally has severe PowerPoint fatigue—will appreciate. All of which makes both you and your presentation more memorable.

## SUMMING IT UP:

- Don't confuse creating your slides with practicing your presentation. Practice. A lot.

- Ensure that the physical elements—table, screen, tech support—are positioned to enhance your message.

- Channel your inner Publishers Clearing House announcer when delivering numbers.

- Make sure each word in a list is given a distinct personality by varying your tonal quality.

- Create margin notes that trigger a story to accompany every slide.

- There are tried-and-true formulas for putting together an effective slide. Include them whenever possible.

- Decide on, and state, your question policy—before, during, or after—at the outset of your meeting or presentation.

- Avoid using "Good question" as filler when considering how to tackle a tough question.

- Props can be even more valuable than pictures. Consider how and when "show and tell" might serve you.

## CHAPTER SEVEN

# Put It in Writing:
## But Before You Do . . .

In these days of instant messaging, text messaging, e-mail, etc, it's easy to forget that writing is an art form. And, as with any art form, people tend to have strong views about what they like and what they don't like, and what they feel is over- and what they feel is under-rated.

My goal in this section is not to set myself up as the arbiter of taste in this arena. My goal is to tell you what I've found effective, what I feel are baseline must-haves, what I love, and what makes me nuts. You, then, can pick and choose what you agree with, and what you think are the leftover hang-ups of an English major (not to mention longtime reader-under-the-covers-when-I-was-meant-to-be-sleeping).

Within this chapter you'll find writing fairly broadly defined. I'll look at the basics: pitch letters, cover letters, résumés, and more. But I'll also tackle scripts for cold calls and RFPs (requests for proposal), both fairly recent phenomena. E-mail etiquette will be considered, as well as the old-fashioned, handwritten, snail mail thank-you note. Broad strokes, such as the importance of keeping a quote file, will be discussed, as will more pointillist issues such as appropriate signage in the restroom. And, finally, I'll inject my idiosyncratic feelings on topics such as the importance of good stationery and the hideousness of the "emoticon."

Ultimately, my hope is that you finish the section with a heightened sense of the power of the written word, and a heightened sense of power in your ability to move others through your writing.

## Being There

Writing is a tricky thing. Many of us have a lot of thoughts and feelings about whether or not we are good at it. What we don't realize is that the majority of the time these thoughts and feelings are often just the mental regurgitation of comments made to us by parents and teachers during our formative years, comments that we filed away in our brains with a label on them saying "truth," without ever stopping to decide if they had merit.

From where I sit, if they are negative, they don't have merit.

Now I'm not saying that I don't differentiate between writing that is fluid, or lapidarian, or incisive, or insert-adjective-here, and writing that doesn't move me as immediately. What I'm saying is that anytime someone has taken the time to authentically put their observations or concerns or sentiments down in writing, it is automatically good because it is achieving its objective—it is making a genuine effort to communicate what that person wanted me to know. And, as with speaking, commitment and authenticity will always win out over technique and flash.

Anne Lamott, one of the many people I consider a mentor-at-one-remove (which is a nice way of saying that I feel certain she'll be one of my absolute best friends if we ever meet) put it best in her book on writing, *Bird by Bird*. She said:

"Write toward vulnerability. Don't worry about appearing sentimental. Worry about being unavailable; worry about being absent or fraudulent."

In other words, as slogans and titles and taglines from books to yoga clothes are telling you, good writing is about being present— opening your mind and your heart and allowing others to see what's inside.

## You Can Quote Me

I've always been a reader. There are countless books I adore and which, if I had to, I could quote from verbatim.

When I began working in publishing—*getting paid to read*—it was nirvana. The trouble, however, was that I was having trouble retaining all the great things I was reading every day. So I opened a quote file: a place where every time I read something I loved, or that I felt summed up a mood or a feeling or a belief, I could write it down and have it handy when my own words felt inadequate.

Ten years later I have quite a quote file (but, obviously, not a more poetic name for it). Thirty-five pages long at the moment, it's my go-to when I need to distill a thought, bolster an argument, or enhance a project. It's also a terrific place to do some creative procrastination when work needs to get done. I often go in with one objective and end up browsing through the "greatest hits" of people I've come to think of as friends, mentors, and role models. In this way, it's its own educational tool. I'll read a snippet of something I think is super-smart or beautifully expressed, and get so excited about it I'll end up reading everything that person has written.

And in this age of the laptop computer, it's absurdly easy. Open the document, type it in, shut it. Bang, it's there when you need it. For instance, it's been invaluable to me as I worked on this book.

So as you begin to think of how you can enhance your written word, think of some quotes that jump to mind: "The only thing we have to fear is fear itself," "Discretion is the better part of valor," "When you want me, just put your lips together and blow," (Okay, maybe not that one) and type them up. You'll be amazed how quickly it becomes habit to drop things in as you hear them or read them. And then, when you're in a creative crunch—you need a lead-in to a speech, you need an inspirational quote to leave on-screen at the end of your PowerPoint presentation, you need an authority to bolster your argument with your colleagues—you'll have eloquent friends to call on.

## The Devil's on E-mail

Setting aside the fact that I could be described as a bit of a techno-phobe, or a "late-adapter" (my brother keeps saying I'd better get it to-gether or he won't let me use his holographic toaster in 2050), I do think e-mail can be a useful tool . . . sometimes . . . in the most utilitarian kind of way.

For example, I think e-mail's great if a meeting time has been changed and I need to let fifteen people know that. Or I want to send out an invitation to a few friends to meet me for a margarita.

What I never, ever think e-mail is useful for is in-depth dialogue—and don't even think about using it for problem solving. You might just as well get out gasoline and a match.

Why? Because e-mail can't convey tone. And, as we've learned, tone accounts for 38 percent of how you are understood. It also, obviously, can't convey physicality, which is 55 percent of how you are understood. . . . So you have a 7 percent chance of being understood using e-mail as a tool.

Those aren't odds I would take.

The other tricky thing about e-mail is that the immediacy of it makes people become both careless and crazy.

Careless when the communication is flowing along—zip, zip, zip—and the next thing you know you're sending out emails that are not only grammatically incorrect or riddled with misspellings, but you've also found you've divulged far, far too much personal information, *and* inadvertently hit "Reply All."

Crazy when you send an e-mail and get no response, at which point it's possible you tell yourself that you *know* he or she has read it; why haven't you gotten a response? And then, often, you begin the internal storytelling process—he must have thought this, she must have felt that . . . It simply wasn't possible that he or she had stepped out to walk around the block, or get a coffee, or meet their mother. No. Their nonresponse was *directly* attributable to your email.

At this point, it can be hard to tell that you've set up your wigwam

## Things That Make Me Go Blechh

As noted, the immediacy and ease of e-mail and instant messaging make it easy for people to get sloppy. What's astounding to me is that it also seems to make people incorporate still more shortcuts. It seems it's not enough to know it will be delivered immediately—they want to make sure it gets read *even faster* and so resort to abbreviations (ttyl, lol, c u soon, g 2 g jump to mind) and the use of emoticons (my fervent prayer is to never again be subjected to a ☺ or a ☹ again—or even : ) or : ( ). Should you be someone who falls back on these, please, please limit them to your personal correspondence. They do not have a place in business.

Not surprisingly, I have similarly strong feelings about "personalizing" e-mails with colored backgrounds or unusual typefaces. Yes, it might make them more memorable. But it's unlikely it will be for a good reason. Elle Woods personalizing her résumé in *Legally Blonde* by making it pink and scented was, in fact, a joke.

And, since we're on the subject of e-mail pet peeves, I'm also going to request that you severely limit your use of exclamation points!!!!!! AND CAPITAL LETTERS. No one likes to be screamed at, in person or by e-mail.

Finally, I love the Dalai Lama as much as the next person, but please don't send along his purported wisdom (or anyone else's) in a chain letter. Likewise, the world's funniest joke or best chocolate chip cookie recipe. Their arrival via e-mail leaves a bad taste in the receiver's inbox.

in Crazy-Town. Consequently, you blast out a second (or third, or fourth . . .) e-mail filled with your dubious guesswork, or view any response you get as either loaded with hidden meaning or violently anticlimactic . . . both of which tend to restart the cycle.

This is not good.

That said, I have succumbed to the idea that my one-woman crusade is not going to end e-mail usage anytime soon. Consequently, I urge you—I implore you—to treat writing any e-mail that is not strictly utilitarian as an unexploded landmine. Once you have written it, not only spell- and grammar-check it, but, if possible, put it in a draft folder for an hour or a day, or send it to a friend and get his or her input, or send it to yourself and see what you think when you open it up.

It can also be helpful to do the AI H.A.L.T. check on yourself—ask yourself, "Am I hungry, angry, lonely, or tired?" If you are, *do not hit Send*. It will not serve you. Speaking from my own experience, being hungry does terrible things to my brain. I once read in a magazine (and, if you wrote this, please let me know because I forgot to source it), "Every unkind word you don't say is a love letter time mails back to you." For me, words to live by. Being lonely kicks the stilts out from under me. And I'm absolutely certain I can feel my IQ falling when I'm tired.

None of these conditions allows me to present my best self. I imagine the same is true for you. So, please, handle e-mail with care.

## When It's Time to Résumé

Many of us have been in our fields for so long that the idea of putting together a résumé feels as foreign as it did when we sat down to write the one that landed us our first job. Often adding to that feeling of disorientation is the fact that changing jobs and/or careers midlife is due to some type of physical, financial, or emotional upheaval—rarely a time you're motivated to sit down and write up a list of your accomplishments and experience.

This said, it has to be done, so here are a few fast reminders of the dos and don'ts of effective résumé writing:

- Do keep it clean and uncluttered. I've noticed that one of the side effects of having to tackle writing a résumé is to spend a lot of time playing with different fonts and spacing. This creative procrastination will leave you with a document that's visually fatiguing to read.
- Do keep it concise. Yes, you have far more accomplishments

than you did starting out, but that doesn't mean your reader
has far more time to read about them. Edit, weed, hit the
highlights.

- I recommend referring to your work history as "Overview of
  Qualifications," rather than "Summary of Work Experience."
  The choice of "overview" as opposed to "summary" em-
  phasizes the above point—that this is simply a list of your
  greatest hits.

- Bulleted points expanding on each qualification should follow.
  For example, your qualification might be: "Extensive public policy experience: this includes bullet point: fact, bullet point: fact,
  bullet point: fact."

- Do use active language. Because much of what you'll be writing
  about happened some time ago, you might tend to think, and
  write, about it in the past tense. Make sure it sounds current.
  Avoid verbiage such as "During this time I developed,
  launched, and marketed . . ." Instead, "Developed, launched,
  and marketed . . ."

- Do give concrete details such as "Brought to market $150 mil-
  lion dollars in product for X," or "During my tenure sales grew
  from X million to Y million."

- Do conclude with a list of any professional affiliations you
  might have. It's possible someone reading your document will
  belong, or wish to belong, to one of them—it's a conversation-
  starter.

- Do plan to tailor your document for every recipient. Different
  readers will have different agendas, or be interested in different
  aspects of your experience. Certainly, each will have highly individual backgrounds of their own that you can play off of.

Yes, getting back in the game can be daunting, but having
a concise, actively languaged, fact-filled, individually tailored résumé in hand will do wonders for bolstering your confidence that
you can, and will, find a situation that's suited to your needs and
talents.

## Cover Art

Writing the letter that accompanies your résumé can often be as confounding as writing your résumé. Packing your credentials into that small space was tricky enough—compressing them into three short paragraphs that are forthright without sounding pushy, confident without sounding arrogant, and relaxed without sounding like a slacker is quite a juggling act. Keeping the following points in mind will make the process easier:

- Open with how their requirements/needs align with your experience/skill set. For example, "I'm writing because the stated parameters of your posted consulting job dovetail exactly with my qualifications and experience. For the last X years I have led a team of Y number of people at a nonprofit firm focusing on Z."
- In your second paragraph, state the reason why you want to move to their firm. For example, "Your firm's focus on X has been a longtime passion of mine./I think your exploration and understanding of Y market represents the future of the field./Your aggressive stance on the importance of innovation and change is one I share." Then, define what you would be bringing to the table. "My experience in X sector complements your current work./My understanding of Y sector will bring added depth to your research./My contacts in Z emerging market will facilitate the implementation of your five-year plan."
- Close with the "housekeeping" details: "My CV is attached. I look forward to hearing from you. Sincerely,"

Plan to write and rewrite this a number of times. Don't try to get it "right" right out of the starting gate. Allow yourself the luxury of being verbose in version one, then pare and fine-tune in your next drafts, remembering always to keep your language active. Ultimately, it should read like a one-two punch, leaving them no choice but to be in touch.

## And Here Comes the Pitch!

We've all had those moments of seeing Post-its or Ugg boots or this week's movie blockbuster and thinking, "But I thought of that *ages* ago." What keeps us from following up on all our good ideas? While there can be any number of reasons, often one of them is the sudden desire to nap when we think of trying to write the pitch letter that will get our idea in front of key decision-makers. Because the fact is that writing a good pitch letter is (to me) as much of an art form as pitching a ninety-mile-an-hour fastball. And, like a baseball pitcher, you need a very particular mix of research, practice, and passion.

First, the research. In the same way a pitcher doesn't use the same pitch on every player, you can't write a one-size-fits-all pitch letter and send it out again and again. Although the bones of the letter can remain the same, it must be tailored to speak to the interests or concerns of the receiver. This requires a certain amount of background sleuthing. Questions you'll want to get answered are:

- What projects or products have they built or published or manufactured or insert-specific-from-your-industry here that piqued your interest in them?
- What is their reputation in their industry and/or in their community?
- Is the person to whom you're writing integral to that project or reputation? How?
- Is there a gap in their product line or blemish on their reputation that you feel your product or skill set can address as no one else's can? Why?

With this information in hand, you can begin writing. The fact that it's a short document doesn't mean you'll be doing less work. It takes a lot of practice to speed a ball past an accomplished player, and it takes a lot of practice to write a letter that will gain you entrée to your target audience—that dazzles in the shortest amount of words possible.

Consequently, your opening line needs to accomplish two objectives: demonstrate you've done the research, and show how you plan to use that research to their advantage. Here's an example:

"Dear X, It's my understanding that your firm is seeking to capture the untapped potential of the 'tween spending market. My idea for a personalized, set-limit credit card redeemable at their favorite stores will enhance revenues from both your customers and your advertisers."

In your next paragraph you want to get into why you've chosen to bring this idea to them instead of one of their competitors. Questions to ask yourself might include:

- Is it because of similar successes they've had in this arena?
- Is it because your sense of their corporate mission is to embrace bold initiatives?
- Is it because their primary competitor has a similar—yet not quite as attractive—option and their standards of excellence have proven they can do better?

Identify for them what you think they will be bringing to the party, and why you think they are the only ones who can do this.

Your final paragraph should be short and sweet, merely addressing the logistics for furthering the conversation. For example, "I will call next week to follow up with you. Should you wish to contact me before then, I can be reached at," then give your telephone information and e-mail address.

In closing, I like to acknowledge that in reading the letter they've already made a contribution. I think this helps to give them an idea of what the tenor of the relationship will be going forward. So, "With thanks for your time and attention. Sincerely,"

## Your Speechwriting Road Map

Everyone has a different way of tackling their speechwriting. Some people like to type it out verbatim, some like bullet points on a page, some prefer index cards. My personal preference is bullet points on a page, for a number of reasons:

If you are reading verbatim from a script there are two ways you might derail. One is that you'll bore your audience, as few of us enjoy being read to after the age of five. Two is that if you're reading from your script while trying to maintain eye contact with your audience you'll lose your place and become flustered.

If you are working from index cards, you'll need to flip through them as you speak, which can be distracting for your audience. Should you drop them, they will need to be put back in order; and even if you've had the foresight to number them, this can take time. Finally—and it's possible this is completely subjective—it can be tough on your audience to see you head up to the podium with a big stack of index cards. Their internal monologue may become something like, "Wow. How long is this going to last?"

So, bullet points on a page. What's the best way to put them together? My recommendation is, bearing in mind your audience profile, to write down every single idea you might have for what you want to say. Don't edit yourself, don't organize your material, just get it down on the page. In my world, this is called the "brain dump."

Once it's down, I recommend taking Charles Osgood's advice and writing your last sentence first. What's your close? This is important in the same way it's important to know where you're headed when you get in the car. It's only after you have your destination in mind that you can begin to explore how to get there.

At this point you can look at the material from your brain dump and choose the three strongest ideas/examples/stories that support your theme or objective and arrange them so that they build on each other, either logically or by intensity of meaning. For example, if you're going to talk to people about getting involved in the charity of your choice, you would choose three examples of the good it has accomplished and arrange them from least to most dramatic, in terms of the number of lives touched or dollars raised.

Then you would think of the "Once upon a time" that would

catch your audience's attention from the get-go and draw them into the journey they're going to experience. This will become your open.

Finally, you will speak what you have *out loud*. This is imperative. If you don't practice out loud, you can believe with all your heart you know how you're going to get from point A to point B but stumble or break down when you get there. It's only through hearing it out loud that you will be able to flesh out the connective tissue. Once you've done this, pick a key idea that will remind you of your choice and make a note of it.

In this way you will end up with a bulleted "script" that adheres to the following basic guideline. For example, if you were giving a speech to the winners of a nationwide recipe contest featuring your product, you might end up with something like:

| | |
|---|---|
| The "Once upon a time": | What caused you to run the contest? |
| | |
| Connective tissue idea: | Criteria for contest |
| Idea A: | Winner had to use our product. And dish must be: |
| | —organic |
| | —able to be made in thirty minutes or less |
| | —family-friendly |
| | |
| Connective tissue idea: | Why these criteria? |
| Idea B: | To expand the public's perception of our brand. Previously perceived as: |
| | —unhealthy |
| | —time-consuming |
| | —high end |
| | |
| Connective tissue idea: | Who/how rose to the challenge |
| Idea C: | We received thousands of entries. Among them: |
| | —biggest missteps |
| | —closest competitors |
| | —why you were chosen |

| | |
|---|---|
| Connective tissue idea: | Your recipes demonstrate the same integrity as our product |
| BIG FINISH | You surpassed every expectation we had. We couldn't have done it without you. |

The beauty of this approach is it keeps you on track, it adheres to the Rule of Three mentioned in Chapter Five, and—by practicing out loud—you will have confidence in your ability to retain your information and so, have energy to give to making the most of your vocal and physical assets.

## Warming Up to Your Cold Call

Like many of you, I run my own business because I love to be my own boss. That said, there are moments when I wish I could outsource some of my "boss activities." Making cold calls to prospective clients used to be one of them. Every time I picked up the phone to put a hit on someone I'd targeted as a prospective client, I'd find something else to do. To paraphrase the Bond film, "tomorrow never came."

Luckily, one thing I enjoy doing is mining people for their expertise, so I called my friend Gregory who adores making cold calls—they actually turn him on. He taught me about writing cold call scripts. These scripts outline in brief exactly why you're calling and what you want. Then they envision every possible negative response you might get to your request for money/a meeting/whatever it is you're seeking and provide you with the rebuttal that will get you in the door. Here's an example of what we put together for a financial client:

| | |
|---|---|
| FCJ: | "Mr. Smith, this is Frances Jones calling from Cole Media Management. (pause) Good morning. (pause) X firm and I have been doing business recently, and I'm |

certain the success I've had with them would benefit your
firm as well.

I'd like to get together to talk.

How's next Tuesday at three?"

Mr. Smith: "What do you do?"

FCJ: "I help executives look better during TV interviews
and boardroom pitches. I'd love to come by your
office and show you how it works. How's next
Tuesday . . ." etc.

As you can see, the body of the script includes *my name* and *the
firm's name*. It includes *the name of a comparable company*—or a
similar enticement—to catch and hold my listener's attention. It includes *a one-sentence description of what I do*. And—very importantly—it includes *a request for a concrete date and time to get
together*. All of these elements should be included in the script you
put together.

Next, we wrote the possible responses I might get and my rebut-
tals:

Mr. Smith: *"I'm not interested."*

FCJ: "Is that because you're too busy?"

Mr. Smith: "Yes."

FCJ: "What are you preparing for?"

Mr. Smith: "I have a few meetings coming up."

FCJ: "Oh, but that's exactly why we should get together. How's
next Tuesday . . ."

Or

Mr. Smith: *"I don't do TV."*

FCJ: "But you do speak in front of large groups?"

Mr. Smith: "Yes."

FCJ: "Oh, but that's exactly why we should get together. How's
next Tuesday . . ."

Or

| Mr. Smith: | *"I have nothing coming up."* |
|---|---|
| FCJ: | "Even better. The less firefighting the better the results—which is why now is the *best* time to get together. How's next Tuesday . . ." |

Or

| Mr. Smith: | *"I don't have the budget."* |
|---|---|
| FCJ: | "The meeting's free. How's next Tuesday . . ." |

Or

| Mr. Smith: | *"I've already been trained."* |
|---|---|
| FCJ: | "Was there any aspect of that training that didn't meet your needs?" |
| Mr. Smith: | "Well, yes . . ." |
| FCJ: | "This is why we really should get together. How's next Tuesday . . ." |

Or

| Mr. Smith: | *"I don't need the help."* |
|---|---|
| FCJ: | "You've never made a presentation you felt could have gone better?" |
| Mr. Smith: | "Well, yes . . ." |
| FCJ: | "This is why we really should get together. How's next Tuesday . . ." |
| Alternate: | |
| Mr. Smith: | "No, *I've never left a meeting feeling it could have gone better.*" |
| FCJ: | "Wow. Then I have a lot to learn from you. How's next Tuesday . . ." |

As you can see, we spent a lot of time (and had a lot of fun) envisioning every possible scenario for refusal, then coming up with a one-sentence way of circling back to my request for a meeting and the "by when" I wanted that meeting to happen. Again, that's an extremely important piece; including a concrete "by when" signals for your listener that you can't be put off with, "I'll check my calendar and get back to you."

If all of this seems incredibly pushy or unnatural to you, that's all the more reason to have a script—so that in the moment you don't blank and back down. Speaking from my own experience, not only did I find these an incredibly helpful jump start to get myself on the phone, but it was unusual for me to hang up without a meeting in place.

## Polishing Your Proposal

Despite the fact that we work at a time when there is ever-greater outsourcing of specialized tasks by large companies to smaller firms, the competition for these outsourced jobs can be fierce. The way in which most large companies weed through the multiple candidates vying for their work is to ask them to submit a proposal outlining their background and their plan for tackling the work. And whether you're getting down on one knee to propose to someone with whom you'd like to share your life, or sending in a proposal to a company with whom you'd like to share your talents, proposals can be nerve-wracking. Given that, I thought I'd outline a few of the elements I include when I send in an RFP, a Request for Proposal:

- Company Bio. The first piece I include is my company's biography: when we were founded, what we've defined as our mission, what this allows us to provide for our clients.
- Experience of Work Team. This includes individual biographies of every person who will be assigned to work on the project: their title, function within the firm, individual area of expertise,

clients with whom/projects on which they have worked, educational background if pertinent (for example, if they have an MBA), etc.

- Related Work: This section includes the names of companies for whom we have done similar work, and the details of what we provided for them.
- Approach: In this section we outline what we understand their request to be and how we plan to address their needs. We generally offer a two-phase plan of attack:
  - Phase One includes an in-depth diagnostic on the company: we interview key staff, analyze their written materials, Web site, etc, assess the current perception of their value in the marketplace as compared to the competition and/ or alternatives, and consider their current internal and external communication methods. Upon completion, we offer some "quick win" recommendations—changes that can be immediately implemented to improve their situation.
  - Phase Two: we put together a strategic plan for going forward. This includes identifying current issues and challenges in their communication and marketing plans, the development of clear and consistent messaging that resonates with both the company and the outside world, a proposed process for disseminating this information to the outside world, and suggestions for the creation of effective vehicles through which this will be disseminated.
- Fees: Lastly, we include the fee we will charge for the work, and recommendations for the benchmarks that will indicate we've adhered to our commitment.

As I said, these are just the broad strokes we use to lay out our background, expertise, and ideas for how we can best meet their needs. Each RFP is slightly different for us, depending on the team we're sending in and the particulars of the potential client's industry and their needs. When you're ready to write—and each time you write—yours, you will no doubt tailor it to suit both your needs and those of the client.

## What a Sticky Web You'll Weave

A lot of people want a visually beautiful Web site. I know I do. To that end they spend a whole lot of time thinking about their graphics and their flash animation and their video clips. And all of these things are important. That said, focusing solely on the visual elements of a Web site, but not the language, is a lot like spending a whole lot of time working on the cover of your book, but not the writing of it. Because the fact remains that it doesn't matter how good-looking a book is if no one's driven to read what's inside it, and it doesn't matter how beautiful a Web site is if nothing drives people to look at it.

There are, of course, companies that specialize in this. The purpose of this essay is just to give you enough information to begin researching the process yourself, or give you enough vocabulary to speak with said companies should you choose to go that route.

How, then, can you activate the mysterious alchemical process known as "Search Engine Optimization"? Well, there are two ways: natural search and pay-per-click.

Natural search requires you to include multiple key words that either replicate, are synonymous with, or are analogous to, the core of the message throughout your body copy as well as in your headline.

For example, if you are writing about the newest wine you're producing in your vineyard in Uruguay, you'd make a lot of references to both Uruguay and wine throughout your body copy as well as your headline. Additionally, you might also reference your proximity to Montevideo because that's a town that comes up when people are thinking about going to Uruguay—it's synonymous in people's minds with the idea of traveling there.

After that, you would want to include as many references as possible to the other marketing you may have done within your profession. If, for example, you had joined the South American Winemakers Association and the Winemakers of the World Association, you would want to include both of those affiliations. (One important note on this is that you need to ensure your marketing efforts don't remain static once they have been posted. They need to be continuously expanded and updated to incorporate the of-the-moment vocabulary people are using to describe your product or location or industry.)

Finally, since you can't pack your body copy full of potential key words because it would be horrible to read, you use a lot of meta tags. Meta tags are hidden tags you attach to elements—the pictures, videos, flash animations—on your site. These key words, or data about the data, that you embed in the programming code are invisible to readers but are visible to the "spiders" that spin their way through the World Wide Web, making connections.

Pay per click is exactly what it sounds like—I think of it as the Web site language version of paying for it vs doing it for love. In other words, you are paying cold, hard cash to the search engine to put your name at the top of the list when anyone types in the key words you've paid for. And, as with most transactions that live in the land of "payment for services rendered," it's up to you how much you want to spend for the services you'd like to receive. More words will cost you more money.

But regardless of the method you choose, the important piece is to know your subject inside and out—both on its own merits and in the context of its competitors—so you can identify the language that will draw others to you.

## Sign Language

As the majority of adults are all too aware, signage has gone from being something we used to see on bulletin and billboards to something we see almost everywhere we look: all over our mass transit systems, in our corner stores, on our hats and T-shirts, etc. The tricky thing about this is that as it's become more pervasive, it seems to have become more sloppy. It's unusual for a day to go by when my attention isn't caught by typos, grammatical errors, or an incongruity of tone that causes me to question the reliability, credibility, and sometimes even the sanity of those in charge.

Here are a few examples of what I mean:

There's a store in my neighborhood that frames prints and drawings that has a sign in the window proudly announcing "Dry mount mating." Needless to say, I will not be taking my Matisse there to be framed, or even my "I heart NY" poster.

I was recently in one of the fancier Hamptons, a part of the world that prides itself on presenting the best to the wealthiest. As I drove past one of the über-upscale markets I noticed a sign in their parking lot that said, "Attention [Name of Store] Customers This Is Not an Entrace," at which point I asked myself, "Who's in charge of the show? How could a commissioned piece of signage with a typo be approved, received, and erected? How could a store that bills itself as bringing its customers the best of the best not correct the mistake the moment it was noticed?" The mystery remains complete.

A sign stating, "Everybody must check your bag," is posted in the window of a teen-focused store near my house. My snarky thought each time I walk by is, "Who is this poor person named Everybody?" It bugs me daily, although I doubt the teen crowd is as particular as they are, sadly, the target audience for the hideously named film of a few years back, *I Can't Hardly Wait*, which I can't hardly imagine ever getting over.

An example of a discrepancy in signage tone and a company's professed image that struck me powerfully occurred in the bathroom of a very posh law firm where I was recently invited to a meeting. I'd arrived to find walls of gleaming wood, conference rooms filled with brass-studded leather chairs, been treated to coffee served in porcelain cups with accompanying creamer and sugar bowl, all served on a sterling silver tray. Imagine my surprise then, when I excused myself to the ladies' room and found the following—"If you sprinkle when you tinkle, please be neat and wipe the seat"—typed up on

Xerox paper and taped to the bathroom stall door. Frankly, I'm still confounded.

Why do these things matter? Because even the smallest discrepancies between what you say you're about and what your signage presents to others can stick in people's minds, causing them to question the rigor of your entire operation. Therefore, signage needs to be word perfect, grammatically correct, and tonally appropriate. Stores and offices that have taken the time to proofread and professionally print any signage, no matter how small it may be—price tags to billboards—project a far more polished face to the world.

## The Writing's on the Wall

Since the time we were toddlers, we've been warned against writing on the wall, with frustrated parents enforcing the law with persistent rule-breakers. Consequently, being told to write on the wall may bring up some traumatic memories of time-outs, withheld snacks, and confiscation of crayons.

It's time to restate your claim as a graffiti artist.

What does this mean? I've discovered that in the same way walking helps us to free up our ideas, while sitting and thinking does not, putting a gigantic piece of poster board or some of the Jack-the-Giant-Killer-sized Post-its on the wall and writing those ideas down does a lot to keep creativity flowing.

Here are two examples:

When one of my clients was beginning to work through the identity for a new brand, we put a lot of the top people in a room and began throwing ideas around. The trouble was that everyone was writing down what they heard when an idea was mentioned—and it's rare we all hear the same thing. This meant that we were spending an enormous amount of time backtracking and clarifying instead of winnowing and moving forward. So I took myself to Staples and bought three gigantic Post-it Self-Stick Table Top Pads (that's the official name, though I like Jack-the-Giant-Killer's Post-its myself), wallpapered the room with them, handed each executive a Magic Marker and said, "When you think it, write it down." Not only did this keep us from further confusion when ideas were suggested, it also freed people up to consider ideas they admitted they wouldn't have considered otherwise, because writing on the wall fosters the outrageous, the daring, the inspirational. From this cocoon of ideas we emerged with a terrific concept for the brand.

When I began writing this book I covered one wall of my office with poster board and divided it up into five sections: ideas, questions for my agent, questions for my editor, dull days (things I could do when I wasn't feeling creative), nuts and bolts. This meant that anytime something struck me I simply walked over to the wall and wrote it down. It was fantastic. It gave me freedom from lists, scribbled thoughts on take-out menus, time spent in the morning trying to remember what I'd thought of the night before that seemed so desperately important that I'd scribbled it on a pad in the dark.

So the next time you've gotten a group together to brainstorm, or you're trying to ride herd on a large project, I recommend redecorating with paper, buying some markers, freeing yourself from the memory of your parents' outraged voices, and writing on the wall.

## "I'd like to thank . . ."

Oh, the obligatory thank-you note . . . that thing that sits on your to-do list like a boil waiting to be lanced. So not the thing you leap out of bed wanting to tackle in the morning.

That said, I recommend you get on it. Immediately.

Why am I so insistent about this? Because, in my experience, receiving a well-written, timely, *snail mail* thank-you note is so surprising to people that the benefits to you are, proportionally, immense.

How am I defining a well-written thank-you note? Well, it has to include far more than the standard, "Thank you for the book (or the blanket, or the ham). It was very thoughtful of you. I look forward to reading it (or using it, or eating it)." Nope. My request is that you both personalize how you intend to enjoy it, and that you take the time—and this is very important—to articulate more than how thoughtful the giver was. I want you to write down exactly what you think the giver's thought process was. For example, "You are so thoughtful to remember how much I enjoy reading murder mysteries to unwind/how much I love this shade of blue/how happy it makes me to be able to entertain friends by cooking for them."

How am I defining timely? Timely is within one to three days of receiving the gift, or enjoying the dinner. Timely means you take the ten minutes—it's only ten minutes—to get it done without a two-week lag time.

Why am I so insistent on snail mail? One reason is that very few people use it these days so it has the advantage of being unexpected, and therefore more memorable. Another reason is that it gives you the opportunity to enhance your thanks by picking out a beautiful card, or using your best stationery. Your gratitude for the present is underlined by these personal touches.

How can you make this process less onerous? My recommendation is that you begin to haunt stationery stores, card aisles, and museum gift shops. The likelihood of thank-you notes getting dropped, or dashed off, when you don't have the supplies you need on-hand when you need them is high. Taking fifteen minutes on a lunch hour, or while waiting for a friend, to pick up a pretty card or a box of handsome note cards, means that when you need to get the note out *today*, you're likely to do it. If you find you're really getting into the spirit of the thing, you can work with a stationery store to personalize note cards or stationery with your initials, name, address, whatever you like best.

All of which means that, at the end of the day, you might enjoy sending the note as much as the recipient enjoys receiving it.

## Dressing It Up

As has been discussed, while words and tone account for part of how your message is received, by far the largest percentage is visual. I bring this up because this idea is just as important to keep in mind when you're ready to write or print your perfectly crafted message. After all, it would be a pity to have all your work undermined by an ill-considered choice of vehicle.

So, how to choose?

In the same way the plethora of models, colors, and price ranges can be overwhelming to consider when buying a new car, the number of choices inherent in choosing your stationery and letterhead can also provoke decision-fatigue. What color paper should you choose? Dead white, winter white, cream, pale blue? What ink? Black, gray, navy, dark green? And how about detailing? Flourishes and swirls or angles and graphics? And what about the "license plate": your name and address or monogram? Do you want a standard-issue DMV plate or the more personal, "vanity" one?

As each of these choices will tell your readers quite a bit about you, and/or your firm, I've included a few guidelines below, as I've discovered there are numerous pitfalls, sand traps, and sheer cliff drops in this seemingly carefree pastime:

- Engraved stationery continues to reign as the "ultimate" in personalized stationery. While the initial cost is often jaw slackening, the printing ever after is far cheaper, as your monogram or name/address plate simply is kept on file and reused.
- Given that, I was counseled by several people to consider long and hard whether to include addresses, spouses, or partners' names on engraved—or even printed—stationery, as these facts do change. . . .
- Request to see the entire alphabet when choosing your typeface, as you may be surprised by the way some letters show up—with a "G" looking like a "Q" for example.
- Gilt in any form = upsetting to many.
- While bold paper and ink color contrasts and lighthearted envelope linings, such as stripes or polka dots, can be fun, you should begin with the stationery equivalent of the perfect black

dress or business suit: black lettering on off-white or navy lettering on light blue. Once these are in your stationery "closet," feel free to branch out.

If someone sends you something you love, keep it on hand to facilitate the conversation when you're ready to sit down with your designer or store manager. Additionally—as with so many things— allow yourself enough time to live with your choice for a day or two before making a final decision.

## SUMMING IT UP:

- Writing from your heart, with conviction, trumps any perfectly grammatically correct effort that has no soul.

- Begin a quote file so that in times of need—speeches, debates, PowerPoint presentations—you have eloquent friends to call on.

- E-mail is great for transmitting facts and figures. Using it in place of in-depth communication, or for problem solving, can go awry.

- Think of your résumé as your calling card; the "greatest hits" of your career. It should be concise, actively languaged, fact-filled, and individually tailored.

- Your cover letter should read like a one-two punch: here's why I'm writing to you, here's what I'm bringing to the party. The objective is to get the interview, not convince the reader to hire you via your letter.

- Pitch letters need to combine the information gathered in your background sleuthing with a description of your future contribution. Write, and rewrite. With these you get one shot.

- Bulleting your speech, rather than writing it word for word, will help you to stay connected to your material and your audience.

- When you have a tough cold call, script every imaginable objection to your offer ahead of time and write the rebuttal. This will help you think on your feet in the moment.

- As more and more companies outsource their work, polishing your proposal is a must each time you bid for a job.

- It doesn't matter how beautiful your Web site is if you haven't tailored its language to drive people to it. Take the time to build in your metadata as well as your visuals.

- Every piece of signage, from price tags to billboards, should be grammatically correct, free of typos, and appropriate in tone.

- Writing on the wall is a great way to free up your creativity.

- Just because thank-you notes are obligatory, doesn't mean they shouldn't be artful. Acknowledge the particulars of both the gift and the thoughtfulness of the giver.

- Be sure you have your "little black dress/suit" of stationery in hand before branching out to more colorful options.

## CHAPTER EIGHT

# Oh So Social:
## Making the Most of Your Social Interactions

For most of us, memories of childhood parties reverberate with joy, or at least a certain hysterical hilarity: ice cream cakes, rides on the Merry-Go-Round, the time your best friend missed the piñata and put the baseball bat through your parents' living room window . . .

Unfortunately, however, many of us have found that joy dissipating over the years. These days, the thought of entering a roomful of our peers having a good time can induce low-level dread. We're concerned about how we look, what we'll wear, what we'll say. Although we realize that social occasions are valuable opportunities to connect with people who can further our dreams and our work, we don't know how to maximize these moments; we're fearful of seeming pushy, opportunistic, needy.

My purpose with this section is to bring back the joy. To help you reconnect with the sense of adventure that used to make the arrival of a party invitation a red-letter day. To offer you the skills to establish ongoing connections with people you think can enhance your life and your business.

Additionally, I'll take a look at social interactions that occur outside the parameters of parties, such as country club and/or co-op board interviews, PTA meetings, school interviews with your children, etc—and parse the moments when many of us feel there's

some sort of "secret handshake" or magic phrase that will gain us entrée into a desired inner sanctum, if only we could figure it out.

Decoding the one, simplifying the other—in both cases my goal
is to instill you with confidence that you have all you need to make a
valuable contribution to any and every social situation.

## Count Your Assets

We've all heard the phrase, "count your blessings," and heaven
knows it's a smart thing to do. This essay's about counting your assets.
I'm not talking about your stock holdings, your super-charged SUV,
or your oceanfront property. I'm talking about the assets you have
that you may not recognize as valuable, and so forget to take pride in
and display.

Why am I talking about this here? Because often I find that one
of the things holding people back in social situations is their perception that they are somehow less than their host or their fellow guests
because they don't have a gazillion dollars in the bank, or a degree
from an Ivy League school, or a children's birthday party complete
with pony rides and petting zoo. This perception hinders them from
presenting their most relaxed, confident, enthusiastic self. Those are
the qualities, however, that actually make a terrific guest.

What are these intangible assets? Here are a few examples from
my team:

My friend John has an extraordinary ability to recognize—and
harder still—articulate why something is beautiful. This asset makes
him a delight to have around because his appreciation is so genuine
and his compliments so on-target. My friend Sarah is a master storyteller. Her ability to capture a group's attention and then get everyone involved in the story inevitably breaks the ice between other
guests. By the time she's finished, it's hard to get a word in edgewise.
My friend Lisa is a fantastic joke-teller, a highly underestimated talent. Her gift for mimicry and comedic timing can make even the
most basic knock-knock joke a crowd-pleaser. And my friend Greg is

a genius on the dance floor, so skillful that he can make any partner look coordinated and at ease.

So the next time you find yourself dreading a social situation because you think you don't measure up in some way, take a moment to consider some of the intangible assets you will surely be bringing to the party. In addition to any or all of the above you might, for example, have an endless willingness to listen, or an ability to draw others out one-on-one, or an unlimited supply of arcane topics with which to dazzle an academic guest.

Henry Wadsworth Longfellow said, "Give what you have. To someone it may be better than you dare to think." Defining your intangible, yet invaluable, assets will help you remember what a wonderful asset you are.

## Your Black Book for Parties

Whether it's signaled by the arrival of an invitation in your mailbox (literal or virtual) or an unexpected phone call, being invited to a cocktail or dinner party can arouse a range of emotions from dread to excitement. If excitement is what you lean toward, congratulations. If dread is your more frequent reaction, know that you aren't alone. I can't tell you how many clients and friends I have who spend the minutes, hours, and days after accepting an invitation trying to come up with plausible excuses for not attending. And contrary to what others may have told you, or you might have told yourself, this doesn't mean you are misanthropic, antisocial, or a "buzz-kill." It means you're human—find me someone who isn't. Putting together a quick black book on the party can go a long way toward making the experience far more enjoyable, however. It can even make it fun.

To do this you are going to have to think of yourself as a cross between James Bond/Mata Hari and Anderson Cooper/Christiane Amanpour, with a bit of your favorite politician thrown in. In other words, you are going to have to do a bit of front-end sleuthing, a bit of on-site campaigning, and a bit of investigative journalism.

On the front end: the invitation will give you a number of clues about what you might be getting into. A fully printed invitation to a party obviously is indicative of far more prior planning on your host's part than a Thursday afternoon phone call for a weekend party. A preprinted invitation with date, time, location, and dress code filled in by hand falls somewhere in between. The formality, or lack thereof, of the invitation doesn't mean you have to be any less prepared, but it does give you insight into your host's mindset and the party's feel. The more elaborate the printing and the earlier you receive it the greater likelihood that, for your host at least, the stakes are high.

Use your RSVP time wisely. If you are unsure about the meaning of "festive dress" send your host an e-mail asking what he or she will be wearing/recommends you wear, and if there are any on-site hazards to be aware of in order to avoid wardrobe malfunctions and ensure your comfort. For example: lawns and dance floors = don't wear your stilettos; "We'll be outside," means bring a sweater or wrap if you tend to get cold and/or wear long sleeves if you tend to attract mosquitoes.

Ask your host if there is anyone in particular he wants you to meet or be sure to speak with. This is an easy way to gauge who you might run into, or to give you an initial focus or objective for the evening.

Don't ask your host for directions. If you're unsure how to get there, check it out online and drive it ahead of time if you have the opportunity and are still uncertain. It's unlikely you'll arrive feeling festive if you've been driving in circles in the dark dressed to the nines, so organize yourself.

I don't recommend asking if you can bring anything—or bringing anything of your own volition. Few things are more distracting to your host than having to stop greeting guests to find a vase for flowers, unwrap a gift, or open a bottle of wine. If you want to send something the next day, however, by all means, do so.

Once you arrive, make it your business to introduce yourself to as many people as you can. If this feels desperately uncomfortable to you, now's the time to think of yourself as a politician who's working to get as many party members as possible to vote for you.

As you join a group, or sit down at the dinner table, immediately introduce yourself to the people on your left and right side. If the width of the table and the flower arrangements permit, then introduce yourself to others around the table.

Once you find yourself in conversation, work to draw others out. The best and easiest way to do this is to ask questions that don't require a yes or no response. I find the question, "How do you know [insert name of host here]?" often gets the ball rolling as it usually involves their telling a story.

And, once the storytelling begins, you're on your way—everyone's just shifted to feeling like they're sitting around a campfire.

## When Your Host . . . Isn't

Every so often you arrive at a party to discover that your host is—for whatever reason—wildly distracted, resulting in anything from forgetting your name, to burning the dinner, to spending the majority of the evening hissing at close compatriots in the corner. My favorite experience of this kind occurred when my date and I were invited to arrive at his client's very fancy country home on a Friday evening, only to discover the guest cottage in which we were staying, while

### No Guts, No Glory

The time to get excited about the party is before you arrive there. In the same way you can't put your feet in a freezing cold ocean to decide if you're ready to go in—you have to commit before touching the water or you'll never do it—you have to commit to having fun at a party in advance. When my friends and I are half-dreading, yet determined, to swim somewhere on the Eastern seaboard on a sunny day in April or May, we yell "No guts, no glory!" before running into the water at breakneck speed. When I'm facing entering a roomful of people I've never seen before in my life, I perform the party equivalent: I make a bet with myself about how many people I can get to know in X amount of time. This choice inevitably helps me flip from dread to anticipation—or at least determination. . . . I'm a competitive soul.

lovely, had no food and we had no transportation. Why didn't we simply head up to the main house? Because our host had very kindly left a "welcome" note saying, "See you tomorrow night for dinner." Hitchhiking to the nearest town was quite an adventure.

But I digress.

In these moments, it's incumbent on you to, as my grandmother used to say, "Make your own fun." Pointing out that your name is actually X, that the lamb's charred, that your host seems to be in distress, will only exacerbate the nutty. Asking, "Is there anything I can do?" while a lovely instinct, is rarely well received. The kindest and most gracious thing you can do in these moments is to put all your effort into charming and being charmed by your fellow guests.

An alternate scenario to the distracted host is the host whom you realize has invited you for the purpose of furthering their own agenda— to set you up on a blind date, to ask you for a loan, to have you verbally gyrate for someone he is trying to impress. In these moments my advice is once again not to draw attention to what's taking place in the moment. Although it can be tempting to access your righteous indignation, it's not the time or the place for a showdown. I recommend instead that you go home *and sleep on it.* This is important. Getting in your car and leaving a scathing voice mail might give you a momentary surge of relief, but it's unlikely you'll be as articulate and considered as you need to be to handle the situation gracefully. Sleeping on it can give you the perspective you need to open the conversation with him by asking, "Why?" instead of "How could you?"

Which can make all the difference the next time you see him on your party circuit.

## Do You Want to Be Right, or Do You Want to Be Friends?

I'm willing to bet that there aren't a lot of people who like being right about things more than I do. And I'm not talking about knowing the correct answer on *Jeopardy*, although that's satisfying, too. I'm talking about the smaller, uglier moments of being right: I was right that we should have turned left half a mile back, I was right that you shouldn't have confronted so-and-so on their childrearing choices, I was right that X band played Y gig on Z date, etc.

This fixation on the rightness of me is an ongoing conversation with some people in my life. My friend David once asked me, "What do you need to celebrate your rightness? A parade? Will that do it?" "No," I told him. "I want a reality show called *Tyrant* where everyone lines up and tells me how right I was about the situation we were in and then I have them beheaded for daring to defy me." (I am, as they say, a work in progress.)

Aside from the fact that it might be hard to get this picked up by the networks—though I bet it could get airtime on cable—why is this a problem? Because what I've discovered, which I'm sure many of you know, is that being right can sometimes have an enormous downside. It can sometimes come at the cost of a business relationship or friendship. This is why, in moments of the certainty of my rightness, I am learning to bite my tongue. This is why, when I remember, I ask myself the question, "Do you want to be right, or do you want to be friends?"

Let me give you an example. A few years ago, I was producing an off-Broadway play with my friend, Clifford. Both of us had been struggling with one of our actors, whom we felt was out of line in ways far too dull to get into here. One day, Clifford called me in particularly high dudgeon. This time our acting chum had gone too far. This time we could prove he was wrong. This time it was *over*.

When he'd wound down a bit, I said, "As much as I hate to admit it, I think this is a 'do we want to be right, or do we want to be friends?' moment. You know how much I love being right but it's possible this just isn't worth it." (As always, it's often easier to give others sage advice than to take it yourself.) A few choice expletives later, he agreed. A few years later, we three are thick as thieves—something we might not have been if we'd gone to the mat with him with our grievances.

Another phrase I try to remember in moments like this comes from two of my favorite authors. Gerald Durrell, the brother of Lawrence Durrell, wrote two books about growing up with his family. In his second, *Birds, Beasts, and Relatives*, the family is once again in the midst of a wrangle, during which their sister says, "You see. I was right." To which Larry replies, "Is it possible that any sister of mine could utter that banal, that imbecilic phrase? Yes, Margo, you were right."

Now while it might have been kinder to phrase it differently, Lawrence Durrell does have a point in that it's rarely necessary for us to point out we were right. More often than not, everybody knows it. Consequently, we'll appear far more graceful—and undoubtedly have far more peaceful lives—if we can refrain from pointing it out when it happens.

I'm working on it.

## Ask Not What Your Country (Club Membership) Can Do for You

One of the benefits of growing older is that the clubs we choose to join have more in the way of amenities than the clubhouses of our youth, which often sported little more than a sign saying "Keep Out" and a menu of multicolored Popsicles filched from our parents' freezers.

What many do have in common, however, are intricate, often mysterious, rituals that must be performed in order to become a member. And, as it was in our youth, these rituals must be performed exactly in order for us to gain access to the inner sanctum. But how can you learn what these are? Who's got the playbook? While every club will have different particulars, here are a few broad strokes that might provide you with guidance:

- If the club you're seeking to join asks you for testimonial letters from current members, do your best to have these letters written by people who don't spend the entirety of their time huddled together in the club bar; it's unlikely the membership committee is seeking to facilitate this "club within the club." Asking for letters from members with a wider variety of alliances and interests will reassure the committee that you mix well with different people.

- Needless to say, you will have put together a black book on the club. Additionally, you will need to do as complete a background check as is humanly possible on every person sitting on the membership committee. How long have they been members? Who is in deep cahoots with another? Who's been making waves? What are their individual interests? Are there any particulars they have been asked to weight more heavily than others, or any demographic they have been tasked with finding? (For example: they are looking for younger members/older members/couples with young children, etc.) While it's unlikely you can change your life to fit their criteria, knowing the criteria exist can be helpful to you as you frame your answers to their questions—help you speak to concerns they might have about your vital stats.

- Finally and, I think, most important, every club wants to feel that you are joining for more than the status or convenience it might bring you. They want to believe you will be an enthusiastic, long-term member. In the same way no college likes to be thought of as your backup school, no club wants to be thought of as your "starter club"—the place you're joining as a stepping stone on your way to the bigger and better club down the road. Nor do they want to be thought of as an extension of your babysitting arrangements, or a name you drop at social functions. They want to know what you plan to bring to the party: that you look forward to sitting on committees, signing up for tournaments, and providing everything from hors d'oeuvres to expertise in the face of anything from a septic tank disaster to a tax audit.

Which is another way they are very much like the clubs of child-hood: they want to believe this friendship is forever.

## Be the One Who "Takes One for the Team"

While the previous section spoke specifically to club interviews, I have coached people for co-op board interviews, nursery school interviews for their children, college interviews for their teenagers. In every case, the same principles can be applied: you'll want to have done an in-depth check on both your entity of choice and the individuals in charge of the decision-making process. These individuals will want to know that you're a good mixer, and that you intend to do more than pay your dues, you intend to get involved—whether that means sitting on the committee to choose fabric for the lobby chairs, volunteering to co-ordinate the door-to-door trick-or-treating, or deciding which cakes are commissioned for the bake sale. If you are interviewing on behalf of your child, the school will want to know that you are both open to their philosophy and that you have a strong family structure on which they can build. If the only reason you want to be in X building or you want your child to be in Y school is so you can tell your friends, or because it's "where everybody lives" or "where everybody goes," it would be to your (not to mention your child's) advantage to find reasons that include community spirit. Finally, with regard to school interviews, if you don't have clear-cut ideas about discipline, television/Internet time, or the priority of homework, etc, it would be best to define them before you're in the principal's hot seat.

## "It's not a choice"

Every so often you'll find yourself in a social situation where you're being pressed to answer questions about yourself, a friend, or an acquaintance that you aren't willing or prepared to discuss. For example, you get asked the inside scoop on your romantic life, your best friend's divorce, or your boss's health. In these moments it can be both nervous-making and seductive to find yourself in such conversational demand, making it easy to get sucked into a conversation you later regret.

Because most of you have the initial good intention not to divulge the gory details, I'm not concerning myself here with your first rebuttal: "I don't want to get into it," or "I'd much rather talk about X," are undoubtedly in your deflect-and-defend repertoire. The trouble, however, comes when people keep pressing. Behavior that would be unimaginable in a business setting—for example, trying to "joke" someone into telling with an "Oh, come on, you know you're dying to talk about it"—is all too frequent when people find themselves off the clock, not to mention with a drink in their hand.

In these moments, it's important to have a fail-safe out. That out is, "It's not a choice."

Why do I think this response is so terrific? Because it avoids having you use either "I" or "you."

For example, if you were to continue with, "I really don't want to discuss it," you leave yourself open to commentary along the lines of the above or, "Well, X said you were speaking to him about it yesterday"—and now you're on defense.

If, however, you move to a "you" statement anywhere in the spectrum from, "Why are you so interested?" to "It's none of your business," you risk getting into a personal confrontation of another kind.

"It's not a choice," keeps you out of both of these conversations.

Of course, you're going to want to keep your tonality light and your body relaxed while you say it. Smiling helps, too. But knowing you have a nondefensive, nonconfrontational out will make this a whole lot easier.

## "May I introduce . . ."

In this day and age of tabloid headlines detailing the "personal lives" of the celebrities-of-the-moment, each referred to solely by their first name—if not the sick-making mishmash of their two names: Bennifer, TomKat, Brangelina—it might seem archaic to refer to someone you don't know, or to whom you have only been introduced, as Mr. or Mrs. So-and-So. I, however, remain a fan of this choice. Whether it's a business or social situation, it is best to err on the side of being too polite.

For example, I was recently working with a team that had been hired to represent two artists, both of whom were no longer alive. Of the team members, only one had known them well before their deaths. In this instance, to refer to them as, say, Jane and Jim, implied a false familiarity with them, in addition to seeming faintly undignified. Given that, we made an across-the-board decision to stick with Mrs. X and Mr. Y when speaking about them to the press and the public.

Speaking from my own experience, I had the great good fortune to work at Doubleday Publishing when Mrs. Onassis was still alive—and this was how I, and the majority of the office, addressed her. Consequently, it was always jarring to have people ask me, "Oh, do you know Jackie O?" when they heard where I worked. This transfer of tabloid headline to human being denied her the dignity she was due.

My recommendation, then, is to open with Mr. or Mrs. when you're introducing yourself to someone whom you don't know for the first time. It's hard to go wrong with, "Excuse me, Mr. Smith, I wanted to introduce myself. My name is Bill Brown." While it's more than likely he'll say, "Nice to meet you. Call me Ted," you've allowed that to remain his prerogative.

In situations where the introduction's being made by a mutual friend you'll follow your friend's lead, of course. If he says, "This is Ted Smith," there's no need for, "Hello, Mr. Smith." A firm handshake and "Hello, Ted, so nice to meet you," will suffice.

# The Ways of Word-of-Mouth Marketing

One of the often unspoken incentives for joining the "right" club, being at the "right" party, belonging to the "right" poker game—even going to the "right" rehab center—is how much marketing gets done in these ostensibly social situations. And while this idea may give some of you the jim-jams, the fact remains that word-of-mouth marketing is a powerful tool should you choose to use it.

For the purposes of this essay, I'm going to assume you choose to use it.

At this point, then, the question becomes: how do you maximize it? How do you manage to talk about what you do without sounding overcompensatory, boastful, or like you're shilling for work?

My first recommendation is that you don't "open" with what you do either by name or by profession. Don't, as you're shaking hands, say, "Hi, I'm Joe Brown. You may have heard of my company, Brown and Sons." Or, "Hi, I'm Ann Smith, I'm in real estate." This is off-putting. It leaves your listener feeling that you aren't interested in getting to know him as much as you are interested in telling him about yourself.

Second, should the person with whom you're speaking in-

## "Hi, My Name Is"

Ah, the "Hi, My Name Is" crack 'n' peel sticker—the obligatory, dry-cleaning-necessitating, often mortification-inducing must-have lapel sticker at many large functions.

My purpose here is not to argue their general usefulness or otherwise (although, not surprisingly, I have a lot of thoughts on this), but to say that, since they are so often de rigueur, it's important to know where to place them: that is on your right lapel.

The reason for this is that we shake hands with our right hand, so having that sticker on your right lapel means that the person to whom you're introducing yourself can look down, get a firm handshake started, then have his eyes travel over your name tag on his way to making eye contact with you. This helps him to easily incorporate your name into his greeting—and making others' lives easier generally means they like you better.

quire about what you do, don't assume it's because he wants to know the details. This question (which is not one I love, by the way, although it's all-pervasive in our culture) is generally just a bridge to general conversation or—and here it's possible I will sound cynical—a prompt for you to inquire what he does.

This prompt is a gift. This prompt is where you can begin to discover the particulars of another's profession. As you listen it's possible you'll hear a mesh with what you do. More likely—and almost more important—however, is the possibility you'll hear a mesh with something you were told by someone at last week's poker night or picnic. And now you have an opportunity to network. Now you have the chance to hook two people up. Now you're playing with the big boys.

Why is hooking other people up important? There are a few reasons. The first, of course, is that it's a generous gesture. How can you go wrong with that? Second, the two people whom you've introduced are now two people who are going to go out into the world and tell others what a super businessperson you are. At this point you have at least three mouths spreading good word of mouth about you. And although I can't do higher math, I do know three is more than one.

In the unlikely event you do hear an immediate opportunity to work with or capitalize on an introduction to someone, don't attempt a full frontal rush in the moment. No matter how terrific the opportunity, it's unlikely you'll leave the party waving a signed contract. Instead, mention to that person that a business-related possibility has occurred to you and ask if you can follow up with him during his business hours sometime in the coming week. Don't, even if you're pressed, attempt a pitch in the moment. Aside from the general inappropriateness of it, the chances of your being interrupted are too great.

Should you get a green light for following up, be sure to inquire the best way to do so. Would he prefer e-mail or telephone? Is there a day of the week or time of the day that's best for him? When you do follow up, keep it businesslike. While it's true you met in a social situation, the playing field has changed. Respect the rules of the home turf.

## Raising a Glass

Many of us have had to give toasts at one time or another—a friend's wedding, a business dinner, an anniversary party—and often we think that because a toast is generally short, and the crowd will have had at least one drink, if not more, we don't have to do that much preparatory work. I'm here to tell you that you do. Or at least you do if you want your toast to be memorable. As with all other public speaking, giving a toast is an art form. Given that, some of the finer points of toast-making follow.

If you are giving a toast at a business event, or a business event masquerading as a social event, it's more than likely you will have to factor in the presence of a number of strong personalities or powerful entities in the room, all of whom need to be acknowledged. Let me give you an example:

One of my clients had been asked to give a toast at a dinner he was giving in his home. The tricky bit was that he was hosting the presidents of two nations: one, a quite powerful nation. The other . . . less so. The challenge, then, was balancing his remarks so everyone received an appropriate yet commensurate level of recognition. It took us six hours, but we got there.

How did we get there? By acknowledging the unique contributions of both players. The more powerful nation was stepping in to bring much-needed financial resources to the region, but the less powerful country had been my client's, and his family's, home for many years. Highlighting his appreciation of how and why he valued the distinct nature of each one's contribution left both feeling appreciated.

The same idea applies when you are giving a toast at a more personal function. Since it's likely you were asked to give the toast because your connection to the person in question is unique, milk that unique element for all it's worth.

For example, my friend David had to give a toast at his brother's wedding. The tricky bit in this instance was that a *New York Times* best-selling author and a well-loved television personality had also been tapped to give toasts—one just before him, one just after. How could he put together something that would stand out?

My advice to him was that since no one there would have the same relationship to his brother that he did, highlighting that connection and building from there was sure to make what he said stand out. Then he remembered realizing that his brother's fiancé was "the one" from various changes in his brother's dating behavior during their courtship. Bingo. Only he would know this, because only he was privy to that inside information. These alterations in his brother's mating rituals became the foundation for a funny, heartfelt, memorable toast.

So, the next time you have to speak at your daughter's wedding, your parents' anniversary, your son's bar mitzvah, consider the (non-embarrassing) ways you might highlight an aspect of the person in question, or an experience you might have shared, and weave those stories or details into your words. Have you shared memorable camping trips? Piano recitals? Vacations? Sporting events? Was there anything that occurred that left you feeling inspired by or proud of that person—or certain those two people were meant to be together? If so, let them know. Everyone will appreciate it.

## Up, Up and Away

Because it would be a pity to have your thought-provoking story, witty commentary, or heartfelt appreciation, fall flat due to less-than-elegant delivery, here are a few pointers on the physicality of giving a memorable toast:

- Rather than clinking silverware against a glass—which drives me wild—simply stand up and move about a foot from the table to get the attention of your guests. The reason for stepping back is that the more people can see of you, the better an impression you'll make. (FYI: the same is true when you arrive at someone's door. After knocking or ringing, step far enough away from the door so that they can see all of you when the door is opened.)

- If it's a larger event, have the waiters circulate with glasses of champagne saying, "These are for the toast X will be giving shortly."

- Don't begin speaking until you have collected the attention of the room. If necessary, prep the waiters beforehand to request that guests quiet down.

- At larger events, such as weddings or bar or bat mitzvahs, be sure not only to tell the guests your name, but also your relationship to the guest of honor, "I'm his college roommate," "I'm her godparent," etc.

- If you are going to acknowledge the efforts of your spouse, friends, or colleagues, be sure to gesture toward them as you say their names. If you feel applause is in order, you begin the clapping.

- If the toast is in honor of a guest of honor, be sure to both acknowledge that person with a gesture at the outset of your toast, and raise your glass toward that person while looking directly at him, at the end.

- After you sit down, acknowledge the congratulations of your dinner partners, or party guests, with a simple "Thank you." No need to get into how glad you are that it's over.

Enjoy the party.


## SUMMING IT UP:

- If a social situation has you feeling overawed, defining your intangible—but utterly valuable—assets ahead of time will boost your confidence and enjoyment.

- Your party black book should combine some front-end sleuthing with some on-site investigative journalism.

- If your host is distracted, make your own fun. Charm, and be charmed by, your fellow guests.

- Sometimes being right isn't worth it. In moments of doubt, ask yourself, "Do I want to be right, or do I want to be friends?"

- When interviewing for a club make sure to get recommendations from a variety of members, know the backgrounds and criteria of the committee, and be genuinely willing to get involved.

- "It's not a choice" is a nondefensive, nonconfrontational way to terminate a conversation you're unwilling to continue.

- The honorific "Mr." or "Mrs." will rarely get you into trouble when introducing yourself to others. It's difficult to err by being too polite.

- Don't attempt a full frontal assault if you meet someone socially whom you feel could be an interesting business contact. Do mention you might follow up with him in a day or two.

- Weaving (nonembarrassing/not overly intimate) stories or memories about the people in question into your toast will help your toast stand out.

- Support your toast-writing efforts by managing both your physicality and crowd control among your guests.

## CHAPTER NINE

# The Fine Points of Verbal Finesse:

## Answers to Questions, and Question and Answer

As you know, we began with a number of overarching, "don't-leave-home-without-them" general principles. To end, we will look at some of the fine points of verbal finesse: the importance of careful language choice, considering the intention of your speaker, and keeping your cool during question and answer.

The purpose of this is to help you further develop your clairaudience: your ability to hear what's not being said as clearly as what is being said—and, having done that, to respond with language that factors in all the spoken and unspoken elements in play.

I focus a lot on question and answer because despite the fact that this is the conversational style most of us use as we move through our lives, I know from my own experience, and that of my clients, that the dread of being asked a question to which we don't know the answer can be overwhelming. It's often, in fact, superseded only by our fear of asking "the wrong question" or "a stupid question"—two things that aren't, in fact, possible if you have the tools to phrase your question in a way that elicits the information you need.

As John Ruskin said, "To be able to ask a question clearly is two-thirds of the way to getting it answered."

Another reason for this focus is that questions are an invaluable tool for clarifying misunderstandings and defusing tense situations. Knowing how and what to ask in moments when the stakes are high can be tricky, however. Parsing the intention of the speaker, and considering questions you might want to ask yourself before you speak, are both great ways to get to the root of what's being thought and said—and sometimes to the disconnect between those two things.

Ultimately, the goal of this section is for you to feel confident that regardless of the situation—one-on-one, as the speaker, on a panel—or the question—meandering, bemusing, upsetting—there is an enormous amount you can do to ensure both you, and your listeners, end your conversations feeling satisfied.

## "You have not converted a man because you have silenced him"

The above quote is from Eldredge Cleaver. I love it.

As important as any answer we give to a question is an understanding, or at least an inkling, of the intention behind the person's asking of it. If we forget to factor that in, we're often speaking at cross purposes from the outset.

There are hundreds of examples of this, from the intimate to the public. Your spouse might ask you if you're going to the gym on Saturday afternoon, intending to invite you to go for a walk or see a movie if you're free. If you're feeling guilty about overindulging during the week, however, chances are you'll hear the question as an implied criticism. If your boss asks what you're planning to do with your vacation time and you're feeling guilty about unfinished reports, chances are you'll hear the question as an implied reproof, etc.

Consequently, our reaction is very overcompensatory, emotionally, verbally, or both. We get embarrassed and—because this feels so uncomfortable—we bluster, we attack, we defend, we apologize . . . we say too much.

In moments like this, the best thing you can do to keep your cool is to stay out of the "Why?" conversation—mentally or verbally.

Don't ask them, and don't ask *yourself*, why they are asking you the question. Additionally, don't assume you know why they are asking the question. Instead stick to a Joe Friday, "just the facts, ma'am" dialogue. "I thought I'd go to the gym. What are you going to do?" "I'm going to see my in-laws this vacation. You?" etc.

More often than not, you'll discover from their response that their question was, in fact, as innocuous as it seemed—that you were the one loading it up with additional significance. The other beauty of this is that should their intention, in fact, be less than straightforward, it has now become their job to ask again in a more pointed manner.

Should you want to, you can take it upon yourself to say to them, "I'm thinking what you're really wanting to ask me is X. Yes? Or am I way off base?" Should you choose this route, the important thing to do after you ask is to actually *listen* to their response—not just wait for them to finish speaking so you can rebut.

This is particularly important for the highly verbal. If words come easily, it's often hard to check that facility and allow others to speak. Instead, we ride roughshod over them, overpowering their objections, comments, or concerns. Which does not mean, as Mr. Cleaver points out, that we have alleviated them.

## There's a Reason It's Called "The Situation Room"

I was a shameless, cracked-out fan of *The West Wing* for any number of reasons. The one that applies here is their use of a "Situation Room" on the show (and, I assume in our White House, in real life).

The point I make to my clients when we talk about this is that it's not called "The Crisis Room" for a reason.

The Persian poet Hafiz says, "The words you speak become the house you live in." I believe this. The minute you label something a crisis, all anyone involved hears is CRISIS CRISIS CRISIS. The adrenaline picks up and people stop thinking big picture. Depending on the personalities involved, some people will begin pointing fingers, others will throw themselves into the breach: clear thinking and possibilities for partnership get lost.

My recommendation, then, is to use the word "situation." A situation is, by definition, containable, and something that can change in response to a shift in the circumstances of the present moment. (The best example I can give of this is when my friend's three-year-old—well-drilled by me—turned to me and said, "I'm having a situation with my diaper.") It's a word where the possibility of transformation to something better exists.

This kind of careful word choice is always important. It's particularly important, however, in today's world of instant messaging and constant e-mails. Because your tone is 38 percent of your impact and your physicality 55 percent, you're really down to the nitty-gritty when you're online—all your recipient has is the words on the page. Given that, it's incredibly easy to ratchet up a situation with an ill-considered word choice.

The other bonus is that you continue to sound in command of the circumstances. Authoritative, calm, focused—everything you want to sound during a "crisis."

### Antiwar? No, Pro-Peace

Rumor has it that a few years before she died, someone asked Mother Teresa if she would come to an Antiwar Rally. No, she's said to have replied, but I'll come to a Peace March.

This kind of sensitivity to the power of language makes me truly happy. This is something I try to incorporate into all my and my clients' words and work.

For example, I was recently working with a client that specializes in producing programs for recovering drug addicts and alcoholics. With Mother Teresa's words in mind we very particularly didn't invite interested parties to join our Anti-Drug Campaign, but to participate in our Recovery Movement.

I invite you to do the same—to look at where you may have unconsciously chosen the negative, and flip it to the positive. You'll be surprised at the change both in your own, and your hearer's, attitude toward your message.

## It's Not an Injury, It's an Opening

As you know, much of your experience of different events depends on your point of view, glass half empty vs glass half full, etc, or on the labels you assign to feelings you have about those events, anxious vs excited, for instance.

"It's not an injury, it's an opening," is a phrase I learned in the Ashtanga community. And while it can be as irritating as all giddy-up in a moment when I've dislocated my shoulder yet again, I've found it lives in the same family as "glass half empty vs glass half full." In other words, if I can maintain enough equilibrium in the aftermath of the dislocation to analyze what I was doing that led to it, not only can I ensure I don't repeat the mistake, but the injury becomes an opportunity to enhance my understanding of what I need to do to make the area stronger than it was before.

I find this distinction between injury and opening particularly helpful when I'm in the midst of, or recovering from, a disagreement or argument with someone. If, in the moment or in the aftermath, I label it an injury, I'm far less likely to recover from it completely and in a timely manner. If, however, I can maintain enough equilibrium to see it as an opening it becomes an opportunity to deepen my understanding of the person or the situation—a gateway for clearer, more authentic communication and a subsequently richer and more collaborative relationship.

I bring this up in this section because successfully negotiating a disagreement is so highly dependent on maintaining, or reestablishing, the question and answer process—both with yourself and with the person with whom you are arguing. And the most important factor in a successful question-and-answer dialogue is maintaining an attitude of genuine inquiry. If you ask your questions already "knowing" what the answer will be, your chances of resolution are slim. If, however, you ask with the intention of honestly wishing to gain a deeper understanding of the other person's point of view or with the sincere desire to understand what you might have contributed to the situation, regardless of how painful it is, you'll be surprised at how much stronger and more resilient your relationship will be going forward.

## "Do you beat your dog?"

The question above is shocking. Questions like these are meant to be—to prompt instinctive denial: "No, I don't beat my dog."

The trouble with this is that tomorrow's headline reads, "X denies beating dog." Yes, that's how fast it happens. And few people bother to read the whole article to find out the back story on the interviewer's question.

These kinds of questions are among the many reasons I am adamant about doing your opposition prep. You have to be prepared for the worst three things you can imagine being asked. You have to have someone you know ask you these questions over and over—in moments when you aren't expecting them—so you become used to stopping and thinking in the moment, not just reacting.

The best way to handle these types of questions is to avoid answering with a yes or a no. For example, in the above instance you might instead answer, "If you look at the charities I support, the ASPCA, the Humane Society, you will see that . . ." etc.

There is, of course, no way to prepare for every possible question. If you are confronted with something you haven't considered, remember Disraeli's maxim, "Never complain, never explain." Keep your answer short and sweet.

One of my favorite examples of this occurred with a publicist I adore. His client was a fashion designer who had said repeatedly that he wouldn't be including fur in his line of clothes. This had elicited all kinds of positive press from animal rights groups across the country. The trouble is that, on the day of the show, half the models were draped in fur.

For many people, this could have presented a large PR problem. Not for this guy. His response, "[The designer] changed his mind." Short and sweet.

## Ouch! That Wasn't Nice

In 1910 Theodore Roosevelt delivered a speech at the Sorbonne in Paris entitled "It is Not the Critic that Counts." I don't have the space to include it in its entirety here (I highly recommend you download it), but the gist of it is that it's far better to take a stand than to stand by and sneer. Mr. Roosevelt says, "It is not the critic who counts; not the man who points out how the strong man stumbles, or where the doer of deeds could have done them better. The credit belongs to the man who is actually in the arena, whose face is marred by dust and sweat and blood; who strives valiantly . . ."

I include this here because it can be very hard to open yourself up to questions about your work or your presentation. While much of the time, the questioner will genuinely be seeking an answer, it sometimes happens that his intention is to show off his own intellect, or his supposed superiority; and he does this by taking potshots at your conclusions or at you—and this can be upsetting.

What do I recommend in this situation? First, to take some advice from the same essay: "Beware of that queer and cheap temptation to pose . . . as the man who has outgrown emotions and beliefs . . ." In other words, don't pretend to yourself that it isn't disconcerting or distressing. Take a moment to acknowledge for yourself whatever feelings come up.

This decision serves two purposes:

> ### "Be a thermostat, not a thermometer"
>
> This phrase comes from Roger Ailes's classic book on communication, *You Are the Message*. I love it and have found it an incredibly useful "verbal visual" when clients are worried about their ability to maintain their equilibrium in contentious situations.
>
> The idea, of course, is that if your questioner tries to ratchet up the temperature with inciting questions or remarks, you don't have to respond in kind. What they say is up to them, but how you respond is up to you—and you are set at seventy degrees and sunny.

First, taking a moment to take it in on a visceral level will help you to respond, rather than react.

Second, should it occur during a meeting or presentation, the moment or two you allow yourself to sit with it won't go unnoticed by your audience. Those seconds of silence are damning. The cheese stands alone.

When you do respond, you might go one of two ways. You can turn the other cheek and offer the bland, "I see our opinions differ," or you can choose to let that person in on a portion of what you're thinking: "I'm sorry you feel the need to attack my work/me. I don't think now is an appropriate time to tackle this. If you'd like to speak with me about this later, I'd be glad to." This combination allows you a safety valve release of some of the emotion you might be feeling in the moment, and gives you time to collect yourself and consider how you'd like to respond.

## "I object!"

Every so often you find yourself in a meeting, or on a committee, where, despite the best intentions of everyone present, the conversation remains circular. . . . You hover just over the solution, but the parameters of the job appear to change each time they are discussed.

In these moments, I've found the fastest way to get things in focus is to give people something to object to, rather than continuing to try to draw them out further. For example if you're on a party-planning committee, instead of saying, "What kind of hors d'oeuvres do you think we should serve?" you might say, "Shall we plan to serve hot or cold hors d'oeuvres?" With that decided, "How many of each?" becomes "Three of each, or four of each?" etc.

The same technique can be helpful if someone's asked a question that's so diffuse you're unclear what you're being asked. In these moments, instead of countering with, "I'm not sure what you're asking me," you might say, "I think what you're asking me is X. Is that correct?"

If it is, you're home free. If not, at least you've narrowed the scope of the inquiry.

## What if?/What *Is*

I have sometimes been accused of "a rush to resolution"—wanting to know how a situation is going to end while still in mid-process. What this evokes in me is the urge to ask several hundred questions along the lines of, "What if X happens?" "But then what if Y happens?"

Aside from the toll this takes on my friends and my mental health, the downside to getting caught up in these kinds of questions within a personal context isn't that great. When transferred to a business context, however, it can be easy to unwittingly detonate a disaster by attempting to answer a "What if?" question.

For example, if you are speaking with your sales team and someone says something along the lines of, "But what if our new Fast-R/Bet-R-EZR product doesn't capture the world's imagination?" Or if you are speaking with a reporter and he asks, "But what if your CEO decides to jump ship?" If this question hasn't been part of your "worst three questions" preparation, you don't want to attempt to answer it on the fly.

In these moments, then, it's important to flag the question as a hypothetical. "What we're talking about today isn't what if, but what is, and what is, is" and from there bridge back to your chosen top line message.

Should your salesperson or journalist exhibit a finely-honed terrier instinct—that is, refusing to let it drop—the fallback position I recommend is, "I'm not going to speculate about X, Y, Z." Please note that phrasing exactly. It's not, "I'm not willing to speculate," which has the potential to be heard as you being nervous about the situation as well, or as you hiding something. "I'm not going to" is strong enough to end the inquiry, conveys authority over the situation or information, and allows you to bridge to, "The purpose of today is X."

## For the Record

Although it's hard to imagine a situation in which you'll be talking to a reporter until you're in that situation, it's worth noting the following: despite any assurances they might give you, there's no such thing as "off the record" when answering their questions.

For the record, this isn't meant to denigrate their integrity. It's just that I've found it best to make this a blanket rule for my clients. While some journalists might, indeed, keep your statement off the record, it's not worth taking the chance that won't be the case. And while you can hire a lawyer and contest it blah, blah, blah, it's far easier not to put yourself in that position in the first place. Even if you have a tape or transcript of the session, or took copious notes that they initialed as being representative of what was said, it becomes your word against theirs—and theirs is already in print.

## Fight the Flab

We all ask, and are asked, hundreds of questions a day ranging in importance from, "Do you want fries with that?" to "Will you marry me?" And while these two questions generally elicit a yes or no response, many times the questions we ask get answered with a lot of useless modifiers. For example the tried and true, "How was your day?" is, more often than not, answered with, "It was good," which, in addition to not answering the question (not to mention being grammatically incorrect—but best not to get me started on the good/fine thing since it drives me *nuts*) gives you no insight into what the person experienced, much less what he is thinking or feeling.

What to do? More often than not an answer of this kind doesn't require you to launch an inquisition; the day was fine, you can move on. There are situations, however, when you need to flag this kind of flabby answer and follow up. Three examples that jump to mind are, "Are you angry with me?" "I'm fine." "What do you mean by that?" "I don't know," and "Do you understand what I just said?" "Sure."

The first thing you want to ascertain is why you think your fellow conversationalist made that choice. Are they distracted, tired, or battle-weary? In these instances letting it drop for the moment will often serve you both best. If, however, you have the sense it's because they are intimidated by the thought of how you might react to their honest answer, it can help you both if you follow up. I understand it can be tempting to let these kinds of nonanswers go, but that choice will often come back to haunt you.

You can tackle this kind of scenario in hundreds of ways, but I've found it's helpful to keep the following three points in mind:

- Don't make it a confrontation. A response such as, "What you're really saying is X" is probably going to end badly. (Note: This is different from, "I think what you're asking me is X. Am I correct?")
- Don't shame them. A response along the lines of, "Do you really understand, or are you just yes-ing me?" will also probably end badly.
- Don't second-guess them. Something in the vein of "Are you really going to do it or are you just agreeing to get me off your back?" will almost surely end with slamming doors.

My suggestion is to instead frame your response in terms of how their answer affected you, and include a reason for why you are asking for more from them. You can almost never go wrong if you move in the direction of, "Can you clarify what you're thinking? It's important for me to know so we can resolve this issue/complete this project," etc.

Alternatively, if you have the sense that they've made a flabby response, their fallback position because their honest answer might be too uncomfortable for them to explore, it can be helpful to talk them through it. (Please note, however, that unless you have a psychiatric degree, your opinion about their answer should generally be kept to yourself.) In these moments, broad questions are generally your best bet. Something along the lines of, "It seems like there might be more to what you're thinking . . ." can reassure them you have the time and the interest to pursue the conversation without tripping an emotional landmine.

## "The fool wonders, the wise man asks"

The above quote is from former British Prime Minister, Benjamin Disraeli. For me, its closest modern equivalent is, "The only stupid question is an unasked question."

While I prefer the more elegant phrasing of Mr. Disraeli, I applaud the sentiment behind both. Even though at times it can be brutally difficult to admit you don't know who someone is, what something is, how to pronounce something, how to do something, etc, you stand a far better chance of being well thought of—and, more importantly, learning something new—if you're willing to ask the question.

Given this, what are some things you can do to feel more comfortable asking questions?

- First: Don't confuse ignorance with stupidity. Just because you don't know how to conjugate French verbs or tie a half hitch slipknot doesn't mean you don't have mastery of numerous other skill sets and bodies of information.
- Second: Point two flows naturally from point one: don't apologize for your ignorance. We all tend to do this and it doesn't serve us, or our listener. Instead, it diverts attention from getting the question answered into massaging one another's egos. Stay on task; just ask the question. If your listener expresses surprise at your not knowing, don't feed into it. Agree and add, "Yes, I don't know. Can you tell me?"
- Third: Remember that everyone loves being an authority. While your boss or your colleague or your date may be surprised by your not knowing something in the moment, this will quickly be superseded by the satisfaction of getting to be the authority.

If the idea of admitting you don't know something still intimidates you, practice asking questions in lower stakes environments first. For example, go to a restaurant serving cuisine with which you aren't familiar and inquire about every dish on the menu that you've never eaten before—go for bonus points by asking if you've pronounced it correctly. Or go into a store specializing in a hobby with which you aren't familiar—golf, chess, camping—and ask the salespeople every question you can think of about what they're selling.

People can be unclear. Directions can be unclear. Situations can be unclear. Asking the question benefits everyone.

## Everything in Moderation

Over the years a few of my clients have been asked to moderate panels, symposiums, etc, in their fields of expertise. Having read that, many of you may consider skipping this essay thinking it doesn't apply to you. Before you do, however, consider how often you have, essentially, been the moderator at family functions such as graduations, reunions, arrangements for weddings or funerals, or during disagreements between family members: brothers and sisters, your teenaged children, etc. For these reasons, I think a moderator's skill set is important for everyone to have, as much of it is cultivating a facility for asking the right question of the right person at the right time.

Before you do, however, you need to set the stage:

One of the first things I tell my clients is that being a good moderator is, essentially, being a good host or hostess. When you're hosting a graduation dinner, you make sure your guests have been introduced to one another. Similarly, when you're moderating, you need to make sure each of your panelists is introduced to one another ahead of time and to the audience at the time. If you notice that over the course of your family reunion one aunt or uncle is perpetually left out of the conversation, you work to draw him or her in. When you're moderating, you need to do the same for an overlooked panelist.

When you're arranging a wedding or funeral the intention—whether to celebrate the couple's future or to honor the life of the person who has died—is usually clear to your guests from the get-go.

When moderating, the intention is often less clear so it's important to state that at the outset. For example, "I look forward to a productive and stimulating discussion."

The reason it's important to set these intentions, whether atmospherically or verbally, at the start of the event is so that if your fellow-planners or panelists get into a heated discussion/argument you can draw them back from the edge by restating that intention. For example, "We're all here for the same reason—because we love X," is a phrase I'm sure many of you have heard at contentious family moments. "The purpose of tonight is for everyone to hear and be heard," is one way of pouring oil on troubled waters during a panel session.

If you're planning a wedding and Great Aunt Flo has begun muttering, "In my day, young people weren't allowed to do X, Y, or Z," you can reel her in by asking for the intention behind her story. "To me it sounds like you're saying you think we're spoiling our child. Is that correct?" will certainly clear the air or make Aunt Flo shut her yap. If you have a panelist whose remarks include, "We don't do it that way at my office/university," you will also most likely clear the air, or liven things up, by asking him a question such as, "To me it sounds like you're saying X's findings are unsubstantiated/sloppy. Is that correct?"

If you do suddenly find yourself in the midst of a contentious family gathering or panel, asking questions that redirect the conversation away from particulars and back to the process will help to defuse the tension. "Let's get back to the seating arrangements. Do you think we should put X next to Y?" can help to short-circuit a catfight about who did what to whom in 1984. "Getting back to our theme—innovation in industry; who do you each admire as an innovator?" will help to bring panelists back to the purpose for the gathering.

And, should the whole evening or event appear to be going to hell in a handbasket, I highly recommend, "What can we all agree on?"

# "Mistakes were made" (Yes, but by who?)

This was a phrase often used by a former client—former because he is no longer in business. Why is he no longer in business? I'm convinced it's due to the overuse of this phrase. He refused to be accountable for any of the missteps, misunderstandings, or mistakes of his firm.

This lack of accountability is something I hear far too often. It's my opinion that if Martha Stewart had said from the beginning, "Yes, I did order my broker to sell those stocks based on information I received ahead of time," that she would have been given a heavy fine and the incident would have been forgotten.

Similarly, the headline in a March 13, 2007, *New York Times* article about the firing of federal prosecutors was, "*Mistakes Made on Prosecutors.*" Within the article, now former—and I believe it was one of the many reasons why—Attorney General Alberto R. Gonzales said, "I acknowledge that mistakes were made here." The reaction from Washington's talking heads? Insistence that Mr. Gonzales step down. What would the reaction have been if he had been willing to personalize his "mistakes were made" statement? I don't know, but I can hope that his willingness to accept responsibility for the behavior of his department would, at the very least, have kept the role of Attorney General from being tarnished.

Why am I so insistent about people being accountable for their actions? Because I have seen over and over that those who are willing to accept the responsibility for mistakes they or their department may have made do more to control the damage than if they had done a "duck and cover."

Let me give you an example from my own life. When I was working in publishing, I had a best-selling author who died. In the flurry that followed that, I authorized the cover of her new book without checking with her estate. When her agent and the representatives from the estate saw it, they were devastated. They felt certain this author would have hated it. Should I have checked with them? Yes. Was it anyone's fault but mine? No. Would it have been easy to have blamed her death and the resulting confusion for my decision? Absolutely. Was that tempting? You bet. Did I do it? No. Instead, I went into my president and said, "This is completely my mistake. I will pay for the new cover and the rush charges, etc, from my own salary." The result of that? The agent called me an hour later to congratulate me on putting my head on the block. From there, the damage was contained.

The purpose of this example is not to set myself up as a hero, or an angel. There are certainly times when I've screwed up and slithered away from the responsibility of the results. But the key word in that sentence is slithered. I felt small, and sneaky for having done it. In addition to the people who didn't much like me for my behavior, I didn't much like myself. And that is, I think, the worst sensation imaginable.

These days when there's a problem in my world, I try to ask myself immediately, "What's my part in this?" The result of this is, inevitably, improved communication and quicker recovery. In the case of my clients, I demand the same accountability. If they aren't willing to step forward and raise their hand when the tough questions start, then it's not possible for us to work together.

The best part of this is that they find, as I've found, that it's a relief to do the right thing—that the bluster and back door maneuvers necessary for dodging responsibility are exhausting mentally and physically. The added bonus—and it's a great one—is that stepping forward is both a time and a reputation saver.

## The Graceful Exit

Every so often you run into a situation where, despite your best efforts to understand and empathize with another, there's nothing you can say that will ameliorate the tension or mollify your questioner. No matter how you come at it, they have a furious rebuttal or caustic remark. In these moments, I've found the best way to handle the situation is to beat a stylish retreat. As is so often the case, however, this can be far more easily said than done.

In these moments, I've found the best transitional/exit line is one I cribbed from Barbara Walters's book, *How to Talk to Practically Anybody About Practically Anything*: "You've obviously given the matter a lot of thought and it's been interesting to hear your views."

If nothing else, should any of the preceding have struck you as a bit outlandish, it's a great response to offer me when we happen to meet.

## SUMMING IT UP:

- When in doubt regarding a question's intention, clarify. Actively listen to the response.

- Considered word choice is critical to containing and resolving "crisis" situations.

- Thinking of arguments as opportunities for greater understanding improves ongoing communication.

- To avoid reacting to an upsetting or hostile question: pause. Then, go to your pre-prepared top line message.

- When asked a confrontational question, allow yourself a moment to feel whatever emotions come up for you. This pause will help you respond, not react.

- If you are having trouble defining the parameters of a problem or question, offer options others can object to, or for what you think is being asked.

- Flag "What if . . . ?" questions as hypothetical. Return to "What is . . ."

- Note flabby responses such as "I'm fine," or "If you say so." If necessary, take the time to clarify.

- People, directions, situations, can be unclear. Asking questions, while sometimes uncomfortable, benefits everyone.

- As a moderator, be inclusive of all, clarify when needed, redirect when necessary.

- Personal accountability is mandatory when tough questions need to be answered.

- Sometimes there is no right answer. In these moments I fall back on, "You've obviously given the matter a lot of thought, and it's been interesting to hear your views."

# Recommended Readings

Ailes, Roger. *You Are the Message: Getting What You Want by Being Who You Are*, Currency/Doubleday, 1988.

Armstrong, Alison A. *Keys to the Kingdom*, PAX Programs, 2003.

Gladwell, Malcolm. *Blink: The Power of Thinking Without Thinking*, Little Brown and Company, 2005.

Gladwell, Malcolm. *The Tipping Point: How Little Things Can Make a Big Difference*, Little Brown and Company, 2000.

Humes, James C. *Speak Like Churchill, Stand Like Lincoln: 21 Powerful Secrets of History's Greatest Speakers*, Prima/Crown Publishing, 2002.

Jones, Judy and Wilson, William. *An Incomplete Education*, Ballantine Books, 1995.

Ladinsky, Daniel. *The Gift: Poems by Hafiz the Great Sufi Master*, Arkana/Penguin, 1999.

Lamott, Anne. *Bird by Bird: Some Instructions on Writing and Life*, Anchor Books, 1994.

Matthews, Chris. *Hardball*, Free Press, 1988.

Morgan, Adam. *Eating the Big Fish: How Challenger Brands Can Compete Against Brand Leaders*, John Wiley, 1999.

McKee, Robert. *Story: Substance, Structure, Style, and the Principles of Screenwriting*, Regan Books, 1997.

Nhat Hanh, Thich. *Peace Is Every Step: The Path of Mindfulness in Everyday Life*, Bantam Books, 1991.

Pressfield, Steven. *The War of Art: Break Through the Blocks and Win Your Inner Creative Battles*, Warner Books, 2002.

Patterson, Kerry; Grenny, Joseph; McMillan, Ron; Switzler, Al. *Crucial Conversations: Tools for Talking When the Stakes Are High*, McGraw Hill, 2002.

Ramanamaharshi, Sri; Godman, David. *Be as You Are: The Teachings of Sri Ramanamaharshi*, Arkana/Penguin, 1989.

Ricks, Thomas E. *Making the Corps*, Touchstone/Simon and Schuster, 1997.

Silbiger, Steven. *The Ten Day MBA: A Step by Step Guide to Mastering the Skills Taught in America's Top Business Schools*, Quill/William Morrow, 1999.

PHOTO: © COSIMO SCIANNA

FRANCES COLE JONES founded Cole Media Management in 1997. The company's focus is to cultivate clients' inherent strengths to develop the powerful communication skills that will enhance their professional and personal performance. Jones's work includes preparation for television and print interviews, IPO road shows, meetings with potential investors, and internal meetings with partners, sales staff, and in-house personnel. She also provides presentation skills seminars and is an accomplished speechwriter. She lives in New York City.